Stories from a Global Cowgirl

"DON'T PUT A CAT ON YOUR HEAD!"

SUNNY McMURTREY

GLOBAL COWGIRL VENTURES

Global Cowgirl Ventures, Frederick, MD
(An initiative of Global Cowgirl LLC)

ISBN: 978-1-7351938-0-9

Cover and interior design: Lynn Amos, Fyne Lyne Ventures LLC

For Daddy, who passed on to me his passion
for telling a story.

For Mother, who passed on to me her attitude of amor fati—
seeing everything that happens in your life, including suffering and
loss, as good or necessary.

Ideally a book would have no order to it,
and the reader would have to discover his own.

Mark Twain

I wish I could show you, when
you
are lonely
or in darkness,
the astonishing light of
your
own being.

Hafiz

TABLE OF CONTENTS

ALL MEAT AND NO GRISTLE

Texans love a story. Sometimes the tale is tall, sometimes it cracks up the funny bone, and it always cuts to the bone of truth. I grow up in Texas listening to my people swap stories about each other and our family's foibles. Should these stories of guts and foolishness take a tiresome turn, my relatives shift their gimlet eyes of observation to what is going on in the rest of the world. They are the poor of Texas. Migrant workers in the oilfields. The richness in their lives doesn't come from money and possessions, but from connecting with the people around them and telling each other the stories of their lives.

What I learn listening to all these stories growing up is that life is not for the frail of heart. Life's survivors and thrivers possess the stubbornness of a donkey and the flexibility of a fishing rod.

When it comes time for me to take on the world, I can't shake my passion for hearing people's stories, so I become a television news producer, journalist, and interviewer. For a fair number of years, I am an off-air reporter and producer for Barbara Walters.

As a cowgirl who never likes being fenced in, I'm a bit of a professional Bedouin. Besides my career in broadcasting, I've also been a private investigator and voice coach. Riding in each of these professional saddles has given me the rare privilege of traveling the world and seeing how different we are on the outside and so much alike on the inside.

Traveling for me is about more than seeing the world far beyond the Lone Star. It's an inside journey that means getting to know the person my spirit is most hankering to fix me up with—*myself.*

Even when I'm not working, I can't stop seeing the world through a storyteller's eyes. Everywhere I look I see a story. For a long time, I kept these stories inside me. They'd pace in my head like caged animals. They wanted, they needed, to be set free. At first, I let the stories out by sharing them with friends. Then they'd be locked back up in my mind. Finally, their roars to be set free forever drive me to write *"Don't Put a Cat on Your Head!"*.

No story in this book is more than 300 words. Two-minutes reading time tops. I've worked hard to make each story all meat and no gristle. Cutting to the bone of the truth that each offers. You may read them in any order you like. After some stories, I've jotted down thoughts or questions they've raised for me. As some of the stories are about my own life, I've shared lessons I may have learned or still need to learn. Then there are the ones most special to me. The stories that leave me silent and in awe of both the stubbornness and the flexibility some of us possess to stand tall in a world where the odds are stacked against us.

When I was three years old, Daddy bought me my first cowgirl outfit. I've still got the scuffed, well-worn boots. They're put out in a special place wherever I live, reminding me of my roots and the family that taught me the importance of watching and listening to the stories that bring the world around us to life. I call myself a "global cowgirl" because I've traveled and lived far beyond the skies of Texas, but no matter where I go, I take the attitude of a cowgirl. An attitude that has nothing to do with Western wear, horses, and rodeos. Instead, it's a boldness that embraces decency and directness, sprinkled with a pinch of willingness to compromise, because life isn't always about getting the other fella to say "calf rope." It's about getting things done right. Trying on new ways to see the world around us. Looking through the eyes of another person and seeing what they see. This is what it takes to survive and thrive in a world that's not for the puny in spirit. I hope each story gives you something you need right now—solace, encouragement, a laugh, a hero to worship, or a fresh way to see the world.

— 1 —

"DON'T PUT A CAT ON YOUR HEAD!"

"Don't put a cat on your head!" Mom yells as I race out to the backyard.

Being three years old and a bit on the contrary side, I grab the local alley cat toughie and put him on my head. This normally ill-tempered tomcat should have chomped off an ear or scratched out my eyes. But Tom must have been tuckered from the night before because he sits on my head as still as a furry log. Legs dangling around my ears.

Thumbing my nose at a parental order has no downside that morning. I seem protected by an invisibility cloak because I parade around the backyard a long time with Tom on my head without being spotted. Divine retribution comes a few weeks later, though, when odd sensations cause me to pick at my head. When the doctor parts my blond locks and waves his black-light wand over my head, my past sin is exposed. *Ringworm!* Jock itch all over my head.

Next thing, my butt's plopped on a pile of phone books in the local barber's chair. Electric clippers scalp off my blonde locks, leaving me with crying blue eyes and a shiny noggin covered in round, pinkish "tats."

But the worst is to come. My cotton-white hair grows in drab brown, and when it pokes out a timid two inches from my head, Mom gives me a *perm*. Then, with front teeth now missing and a kinky mat of dark hair, I'm taken to Sears for a photo op in the yodeling outfit Mom's made me. I look like a little Alan Dershowitz in drag.

All these years later, it's still only the bottle that can bring my spirit comfort after that trauma—a good vintage bottle of blond hair dye.

LESSON

This was the day the cowgirl in me was born. I learned to hike your leg on authority and own the consequences. Scratching that itch to put a cat on my head and defying that ultimate of authority figures—one's mother—is a feeling of power that's never left me. I decided to cut my own path that morning. Had a fine time doing it, too. And when the dire consequence of getting my head shaved presented itself, I learned the importance of thinking things through before scratching an itch I want to satisfy.

The cowgirl born in me that day also came to understand that the willingness to hike a leg on authority is a strength that's needed if we're going to right the wrongs and the laws imposed by the small-minded and mean-spirited to keep others down. It's this attitude that lets you live a life that puts you on the side of right and keeps your ledger with God in the black. Consequences be damned.

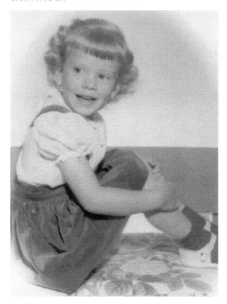

Before putting that cat on my head.

Paying the price.

— 2 —

LOVE AT FIRST LIGHT

When I was three years old, I would perch in a small mimosa tree in our front yard. I was an only child in a neighborhood with no other children. But, up in that mimosa, I was never alone. Most days, large clouds entertained me with a parade of animals and sky flowers; or the clouds would turn a bilious green, warning me to run for cover because a storm was coming.

Then there were the days with no clouds at all and the sky was a white-hot blue. Those were the days when a miraculous Light appeared and swaddled me in its care and comfort. For me, the Light was love at first sight.

Even when the Light chose to remain invisible to my eye, I knew it was there by the safety I felt. There was no worry the Light couldn't take away. I could tell it the good and bad of me without fear. The Light's only purpose was to be my Friend.

When I grew too big to sit among the tiny branches, I also thought I was too big to need my Friend. I was wrong. Again, and again, in the hardest of times, the Light always appears. There comes a moment when it bathes me in its peace and love that is beyond human description. It pierces through my tears and fears and brings me the miracle I most need.

Rumi, the 13th century Persian poet wrote: *The wound is where the light enters you.* Where I once saw my struggles as black and troubling, I now see each as a moment of transfiguration. And I remember the love and peace in each. When my wound lets the Light enter me again.

— **3** —

HEART SONG

"Come with me, young lady. I'm taking you to a place beyond your imagination."

There, in the middle of a dark room, is a cozy chair swaddled in a single beam of light. Back in the shadows is the fuzzy outline of something inanimate giving off the whiff of a faint glow.

"Please, take a seat."

The seduction of the chair's soft padding is heightened by the coarse texture of its upholstery against my palms. Not knowing what to expect, I draw in a breath. Suddenly, the overwhelming sound of music radiates from deep inside my heart, moving out to my ears.

I inhale what feels like the first breath I've ever taken.

For the next ten minutes I sit feeling the vibration of the music start in my heart, then make its way out to my ears, where the vibration is transformed into melody. The clarity of the sound lets each instrument in the orchestra expand to its full potential.

This magical room is outfitted with vintage McIntosh stereo equipment, including an amplifier whose tubes are giving off the glow behind the chair. The acoustic geniuses at McIntosh know how we should experience sound. I am hearing the music from the inside out, not the outside in.

The moments I spend in that chair forever transform my relationship to life. I now understand that a real connection with life never comes from anything outside me, no matter how comfy and consoling that fellowship might be. I know, instead, to listen to the promptings of my heart . . . the ones that become music to my ears. Sometimes the tempo and progression of the notes counter my earthbound expectations, but the beguiling sound always takes me to a place more beautiful than I can dream of on my own.

— 4 —

BAGHDAD

I draw back the blackout curtains and pull open the sliding door. The sun's glare blurs my vision. My skin burns in the rising heat. It's barely five in the morning. *I love it!* I'm reminded of blistering summer mornings in Texas.

I look down at the river below my balcony, the Tigris River in Baghdad, Iraq. Morning prayers from the domed mosque across the river fill the air.

The sun, the heat, the river, the mosque, the prayers—I feel I've come home. No matter I'm Christian with a suitcase full of western clothes.

A cousin who lived here for many years says he and his wife feel the same about Iraq.

"My company sent us to Paris on assignment for a year. Felt like a hardship tour."

That was a Baghdad long before the city it is today. Saddam Hussein was in power, and I'll say, without minimizing the horror of his rule, it was generally safe for Christians. No dress restrictions for me then. Modern hotels. Wine could be served.

Beneath the carnage we now see in Baghdad, and in much of the Middle East, is the Fertile Crescent. A land in which women had equal rights; a place where they could own land and businesses. They were brewers and priestesses; they could file for divorce. The world's oldest wheels were found here. The people of the Fertile Crescent gave us writing, mathematics, astronomy, glass, irrigation, and wind power. The first cities, as we know them today, began in this region. Their stories were rewritten and help form the Christian Old Testament.

Today, underneath the blood-soaked earth of Iraq is a land that gave birth to us. I'm very sad that I'll likely never return to this extraordinary place that has given the world so much.

— **5** —

FREEDOM FROM BIGOTRY BOUGHT FOR A PENNY

This story is more than three hundred words. I want to share it because we are living in a time of fear and rising bigotry. It seems important to remember that unkindness hurts and is at odds with innate human decency.

The lowly penny. What can this modest coin buy you? At three years old, it buys me my freedom from bigotry.

It's in the South in the 1950s. One morning, while at the grocery store with my parents, I inch ahead to watch as customers in front of us pay for what they want to buy. I call where we are a "grocery store" because this is long before the days of giant supermarkets, where you place your items on a moving belt and see them whisked away to be scanned by a cashier. And there is certainly no such thing as self-service checkout. Grocery stores are intimate places. You know your cashier, and you chat with the folks standing around you, even if they're total strangers. Anything anyone says is heard by one and all.

No moving belt means people put what they want to buy on a ledge where the cashier can take each item and ring it up. After she finishes ringing up the man at the head of the line, I push forward to watch him reach into a pocket to get his money. As he pulls out his folded bills, a penny drops on the counter where his food had been. I want to help, so I stretch on my tiptoes to put my finger on the penny and push it closer for him to reach.

Suddenly, a big hand grabs mine, and from behind me I hear, "Don't touch that! Don't touch nothin' a n***** has touched!"

I freeze. I don't know what that word means, but I know the man attached to the hand that's grabbed mine means business. As I look at what I'm told is an untouchable penny, the coin takes on a sparkling white glow. Then a thin shaft of golden Light shoots up from the coin. It happens so fast, and the Light is so bright, that my vision explodes and blurs. The Light seems to burn right through my eyes into my brain and down into my body.

For a few seconds I stand transfixed, my tiny finger refusing to retract from its position over the penny. Then I look up at the face of the man the penny belongs to. He looks down at me. Even a three-year-old knows what hurt looks like.

The man's brown eyes have a deep, moist kindness in them, but there is an even deeper look of pain and humiliation. Whatever that word means, I know it really hurts his feelings. I keep looking straight into his eyes because I don't want to look back at the man who's grabbed my hand. I certainly know better than to talk back to the stranger, but I think, *You're not a very nice man. Didn't your mother ever teach you not to call people names that hurt their feelings? Someone needs to wash your mouth out with soap!*

I hope the man looking down at me can see how sorry I am that the other man has been so mean. When I get older, I come to understand what happened that day in the grocery line. I was introduced to bigotry and racism.

I say at the beginning of this story my freedom from bigotry was bought with a single penny that day, and it's true. Throughout my childhood, every time I heard the "n-word" or witnessed any kind of discrimination, I remembered the Light shining up from that penny and the pain in the black man's eyes. The Light from that modest coin gave me a priceless gift—being able to see the world differently from so many others around me. It relieved me of the burden of fearing and hating another person because we look or seem different from each other in any way.

LESSON

It's a timeless lesson, but one that's taken me a long to time to accept. Bigots of any stripe are frightened people who need our compassion. You can't reason someone out of their fear and bigotry. Only a moment of divine intervention will let them see the world is a safe place. To understand that just because someone looks different or thinks differently from you, those differences don't make them the enemy. That said, until such time as every bigot is bonked on the head by divine intervention, we need laws to protect us from the twisted ways bigots treat the people they're afraid of.

— 6 —

BATTLEFIELD OF PEACE

Peace. Countries around the world search for peace with guns and megaweapons drawn. We've even got war colleges dedicated to developing new ways to fight for peace. All of this done in the hope of achieving this elusive human yearning.

While my own life is full of vexations, frustrations, and anything but peace, I've found a place where I can feel and even "see" the peace I ache to experience all the time.

Ironically, the spot is on a battlefield where the bloodiest single day of fighting in American history took place. September 17, 1862. The Civil War's Battle of Antietam, near Sharpsburg, Maryland.

Antietam Creek ran red with the blood of Union and Confederate soldiers. Over twenty-three thousand were killed, wounded, or missing.

There is a bridge that runs over Antietam Creek—Burnside Bridge. When I stand in the center of the bridge, I see a delicate cloud coming up from the earth, blanketing battlefield and creek. Within the cloud's mist swirls a Light not of this world. Looking into the mist, my mind and body go calm. All worries evaporate. The air is pure, and with each breath, I'm filled with the cloud's peace. I see the misty cloud and feel its serenity every time I stand on Burnside Bridge.

There is something else. I sense the presence of the soldiers who died here, Union and Confederate. There is no rancor between them. Each body released its soul, and these thousands of souls made a peace among themselves that is beyond our understanding here on earth. They rest in harmony at Antietam.

I return again and again to Burnside Bridge to feel the unfettered peace that stretches out to enfold and caress its visitors, no matter the horror of our personal or political battlefields.

LESSON

I believe Peace is the state we come from, and Peace is where we return. Purpose determines outcome. When Peace is our true purpose on Earth, then we will have it. The proof is always in the pudding. I believe this is true in all areas of our lives. When I want to know what my true purpose is in any circumstance, all I need to do is look around and see what I have in my life.

Burnside Bridge

— 7 —

WHOOPI GOLDBERG

Whoopi Goldberg doesn't know me, but I feel an unbreakable connection to her because she taught me the power of kindness.

Wanna big hug from rejection? Be a broadcast producer getting sound bites from famous folks at a glitzy do. Understandably, the relationship between the press and famous somebodies is dodgy. The media are often boundary-challenged when covering icons, heroes, and celebrity royalty. Put us at a shindig where famed invitees are expecting to have some unguarded fun, sans media party crashers, and we're as welcome as salmonella in the hors d'oeuvres.

Tonight, I'm covering such a glitzy shindig. Everywhere I look there's a megamillion-dollar Hollywood alchemist, whose face can turn thin air into box office gold. I feel like a rotten tomato splattering on each famous person I approach with the camera crew. Some show us their backs. Most know the drill and oblige with a few begrudging words.

When I see Whoopi Goldberg, the crew and I charge in her direction. Whoopi sees us coming. I gird for a snub or eye roll.

What's that? A smile? me dares to think.

"Hi there," she says. "How are you guys doing tonight? What can I do for you?"

For five minutes we chat about the event. It's not what Whoopi says that impresses me. It's the kindness in her voice and an understanding in her eyes that says, "I know your job's not easy. There's no reason we can't be friends for a few minutes and talk about this great evening."

Whoopi blankets the crew and me in a glow of genuine kindness and warmth.

Not wanting to sully our moments with her, I call it a wrap for the evening. Neither the crew nor I want to taint the nice feeling she leaves us with.

A POSTSCRIPT

Those few moments with Whoopi Goldberg happened nearly thirty years ago. She doesn't remember me, but I'll never forget her.

— 8 —

OINTMENT FOR AN ITCH

I read two interesting quotes just a few days apart. The first I saw on a t-shirt:

I used to be a people person . . . but people ruined that for me.

It makes me chuckle, that quote, because it pretty much sums up how I can feel about my fellow humans many days. It's not a good feeling. In fact, when someone gets up my nose and my feelings turn less than warm and furry about them, my skin literally starts to itch, a bad itch I can't scratch away, because I know we're not meant to feel that way about each other.

Then I read this passage. A passage that's an ointment for my itch:

Genius

A writer arrived at the monastery to write a book about the Master.

"People say you are a genius. Are you?" he asked.

"You might say so," said the Master, none too modestly.

"And what makes one a genius?"

"The ability to recognize."

"Recognize what?"

"The butterfly in a caterpillar; the eagle in an egg; the saint in a selfish human being."

—Anthony de Mello, SJ

Now, when the itch of ill will toward another person overtakes me, I silently say this prayer: "Please transform me into a genius."

— **9** —

PATH TO THE HEART

Summer vacations for my family begin long before we pack the car and hit the road. When the calendar flips to April, Mother and Daddy unfurl the maps (no GPS back then) and begin planning our road trip. Thanks to them I never whine, "Are we there yet?" They always pick the scenic route, so there's lots to keep me pointing and loving the drive.

When I'm ten years old, we head for Yellowstone National Park. I can't wait to help pitch our tent, make the campfire, and roast weenies. And I've saved up all winter for a Brownie camera (no smartphone cameras then, either) to catch Old Faithful showing off for us tourists. But turns out, the picture I most remember is the one my soul snaps and my heart still carries.

Our journey to Yellowstone includes taking a side trip to see the Chapel of the Transfiguration outside Jackson, Wyoming. Itching to get to Yellowstone and see a few of Yogi Bear's brethren, I hope a good pout might change my parents' minds. It doesn't. Feet dragging and head down, I dally behind my parents as we walk the path to the chapel. It isn't until we're inside that I lift my head. My breathing stops. Before me is a spindly wooden cross on a plain altar. Dead center behind them, a large plate-glass window frames a single snow-capped mountain in the Grand Tetons. The moment shines with a Light no camera can capture.

In that instant, Mother Nature shows me the Light that christens every creature, plant, and object here and in worlds we've not yet discovered. The moment tethers me to the certainty that everyone and everything, seen and unseen, is swaddled in this Light's love.

— 10 —

WHAT'S NEXT AFTER WE DIE?

"My Christian church told me all about life after death and what happens to us." Then Missy almost drowns and has a near-death experience.

Missy explains the experience this way:

There is no tunnel of Light. No consoling counsel from my Maker. Instead, I'm taken on a "life review" where I walk through my life, not as an "observer," but as an "experiencer" of every feeling I've caused in another person or animal. The good and bad feelings.

If I yelled at a customer service rep who then went home and beat his child because my yelling made him feel low, I feel the pain of the beating, his upset feelings, and the child's. If his child later took out her pain on the family's dog, I feel the animal's beating.

We also "live" the long-term consequences of our actions. If you're on an assembly line building a car model you suspect is killing some people because of faulty air bags and you don't blow the whistle, you likely won't get convicted of murder on Earth, but in your life review, you experience all the deaths and the effects on those left behind.

Of course, you experience the good feelings you cause, but believe me: the ill effects of your actions are not soon forgotten.

There is one tender mercy in this. After your life review, you must forgive yourself. "Hell" is when you refuse to forgive yourself.

Missy says there is much more to what she was shown about life after death, but this is what's had the greatest impact on how she lives life today. She carefully weighs every action and how it will play in the made-for-TV movie she'll have to binge watch about her life when she fully crosses over.

LESSON

Wish I'd known about this "life review" business before I was a geezer. Might have done a few things differently. I'd rather be binge watching a "life review" on Heaven's Hallmark Channel than on a channel more suitable for airing "Game of Thrones."

GRAPES OF SHARING

Living alongside a road. Making a car the family home. Shanty shacks plastered with newspaper to keep out the cold. This is my family's history. My grandparents raised two kids in these *Grapes of Wrath* circumstances, as did so many during the Great Depression.

Scarcity walked beside my grandparents every step of their way into old age. Franklin Delano Roosevelt threw those like Grandmother and Granddaddy a lifeline when he fought for Social Security. They had little money for retirement, even though Granddaddy worked eighteen hours a day for decades in the Texas oilfields. FDR made it possible for them to have food on the table and a roof over their heads when Granddaddy couldn't work anymore.

President Roosevelt and Social Security brought my grandparents more than the blessing of a financial security they'd never known all the years my grandfather worked in the fields. The modest check they received each month covered all their needs and gave them a bit extra to put in the bank, and nothing cheered my grandparents more than sharing their good fortune.

Their biggest joy? Welcoming friends, family, new acquaintances—and any strangers who wanted to come along—into their home for Sunday dinner. Grandmother always cooked more than anyone could eat. She hummed as she cooked and beamed as the table filled with "a mess of fresh vegetables," bowls of fruit (a treat unheard of in migrant camps), meats swaddled in the love of delicious seasonings and gravies, and enough desserts to satisfy any sweet hankering you might have.

Living rough in the migrant fields could have cooked all the goodness out of my grandparents. But it didn't. Grandmother and Granddaddy relished the joy of having enough food to cook and share with anyone who wanted to join their table.

LESSON

I want to be like Grandmother and Granddaddy. I want the rough times in my life to be the seasoning that brings out the best in me.

Their lives were hard, but not their hearts.

NEAR-DEATH EXPERIENCE WITH EYES WIDE OPEN

The teenager puts the .357 Magnum kissing distance from my face. We're on a street in Cairo.

Just before the boy walks over to the open window of the car where I sit, I notice a change in the light around me. Trees, homes, lawns, even the air shine with an iridescent glow. All sound evaporates. Nestled in that silence and Light, a radiant Peace wraps me in its arms.

I've seen what a .357 does when shot at close range. I don't want to see him pull the trigger, so I turn to face the passenger's window. Unfortunately, the window is up, and I see our reflections. His finger tenses. In that instant I think, *If you pull that trigger, will killing me heal the pain that's driven you to this moment?*

I feel no hatred nor fear. Then, almost like I'm sending him a mental message, I think, *You are already forgiven, even if you kill me.* With that thought, the teen pulls his hand back and walks away—never looking back. The iridescent Light around me fades. All sound returns. But the Peace inside me remains.

Later that night I go to a neighborhood where there are other young men like the teen with the gun. There are alleyways lined with single-room concrete huts with doorways, but no doors for privacy. Children play in open sewage troughs. I've no doubt this is how the young man with the gun lives—in inhumane conditions with no power to change his future.

I never suffer a moment's trauma from what happened in Cairo. The Light I saw, the Peace I felt, and the message of God's forgiveness for anything we do are divine offerings I never expected from that moment with a gunman.

A GIFT

   Inside what I call the Bubble of Light that surrounded the teen and me, we were swaddled in a moment of Peace that has the power to heal all disagreements and make compromises possible, even between the deepest of enemies. It's a moment that later compels me to devise a way to release the power of the Bubble of Light in our everyday lives whenever it's needed—to help settle the minor squabbles and the big rifts that divide us, to heal what ails you mentally or physically, or to help you start over when the odds don't seem to be in your favor. My experience inside the Bubble of Light with the gunman convinces me the Light has the power even to heal a nation, and a world, brought low by a pandemic. Please go to www.global-cowgirl.com to explore how to release the power of the Bubble of Light anytime, anywhere.

— 13 —

MORE ABOUT THE GUNMAN IN CAIRO

I'm in Cairo covering a news story, the assassination of Anwar Sadat. Teenage boys with weapons are everywhere. A gaggle stands about twenty yards from where I'm sitting in a car near the presidential palace. One of the young men breaks away. He doesn't appear to have a gun. Then, when he stands right next to the driver's window, he pulls a .357 Magnum from his brown, tattered, and soiled polyester pants and puts it to my face. An inexplicable Peace washes my brain clean of normal thinking. My mind expands like an accordion, and I begin to experience many thoughts at once.

One thought is marked in yellow highlighter:

My death, while important to family, won't register a blip on the news radar. If I were famous, I'd be a headline, celebrated with a memorial service. If I were a victim in a mass shooting, SWAT teams of reporters, first responders, and law enforcement would descend on the scene. Mountains of flowers, an ocean of lit candles would mark the spot of my passing, as well as those of the other victims. But someone unknown, all alone? Sorry, not on the press's or the public's radar. I rank right up there with raccoon roadkill.

In that moment, life makes sure I get a good dose of what it's like to feel unimportant to the world, unworthy of attention or being heard. All these years later, I can't get out of my head thoughts of the legions of people standing on the sidelines of life kicking stones and feeling like roadkill.

Perhaps that's why terrorists and mass shooters do the unthinkable. To have one moment, however horribly and tragically misguided, when the world acknowledges their existence.

—— **14** ——

MANTRA OF SUNSHINE AND REDWOODS

Redwood trees took root on earth nearly a quarter-of-a-billion years ago. We've only been roaming the old stomping grounds of dinosaurs for about 200,000 years. Standing at the base of a redwood tree out West, I think of how differently we humans see our beauty to that of a redwood. We like our waistlines to be svelte, nicely tapered, yet we're in awe of a redwood's twenty-foot-plus girth. We spend billions of dollars a year on beauty products and shun the sun hoping to look forever young. The sun is the redwood's pal, nurturing and encouraging it to one day blow out 2,000 candles on its birthday cake.

Lesley, a colleague, sees redwoods as old friends, taking the time to visit them whenever she's on the West Coast. She relishes the grand silence of the forest as she walks among these giants, the duff under her feet absorbing all sound.

Lesley says, "Usually the branches of the redwoods form a canopy high above me, but, one day I unexpectantly happen upon a sun-filled grove. Standing in the middle of the clearing, I look up and see myself encircled by a ring of these natural wonders. The sun beams down a Light filled with shimmering flecks swirling around me. So thick, the flecks are like iridescent dust covering me.

"Suddenly, I feel at one with every person who's ever come to this spot. Every tree that has rooted here. Thousands of redwoods, thousands of people, for thousands of years coming together inside me as one.

"Now, when I meditate, my mantra isn't one of words. Instead, it's remembering the feeling of standing in the grove swaddled in the presence of every redwood and every person who's stood in that grove, covered in the sun's iridescent Light."

— 15 —

GUILTY CONSCIENCE

Jessie and I are ten-year-old tomboys looking to best the guys in their naughty Halloween shenanigans. We're trying to come up with something other than toilet papering someone's house. We wanna make someone jump out of their skin. Scare 'em witless.

"Let's scratch on someone's bedroom screens after midnight. That'll frighten 'em," glees Jessie.

"What will we scratch the screens with?" I say.

"Nails," Jessie says.

So, we skulk out in the wee hours and do the deed. Big success. Folks scream. Wits are rattled. But now our target is PO'd about the torn screens. The whole neighborhood joins the effort to find and punish the culprits.

Based on no real evidence, Jack, the neighborhood sociopath, gets the blame. He looks clean cut, but by the time Jack is counting ten candles on his birthday cake, everyone knows you don't want Jack around your kittens or puppies.

Neighbors are ready to put a stake through Jack's heart. Authorities are dangling handcuffs to escort him back to reform school. All this is too much for Jack's mom. She has a nervous breakdown.

Jessie and I hadn't seen this coming. I'm sick with guilt. If I confess, I'll be doing hard time at home. If I don't, Jack likely faces time for a crime he didn't do, and his mom is left a broken woman.

I confess. Make no excuses. Prepare for punishment.

Jack's mom weeps. She's not mad. She's relieved. Jack just shrugs. He's ridden in the "take the blame for something I didn't do" rodeo before. Daddy? He replaces the neighbor's screens, and says to me, "Did you learn your lesson?"

"Yes sir."

"Are you disappointed in yourself?"

"Yes sir."

Daddy never mentions it again.

His silence was more painful than any welt from a belt.

MORE THAN ONE LESSON

Just as there is nothing new under the sun, there are no new lessons, but your first time learning a lesson can leave a real impression. The cowgirl in me took away two lessons from this shame-filled moment in my childhood. One, there is no greater disappointment than the one you bring on yourself. Two, fess up when you do something wrong, and be proud of yourself for doing that, because that pride may make the anguish of a guilty conscience easier to bear.

By the way, Jessie scoffed at confessing. A real friend—and cowgirl—wouldn't do that. I moved on to better and more honorable friends.

— 16 —

BULLYING

All the news about school bullying has me thinking about Mary. She sat behind me in second grade, and there is something about Mary I can't forget.

Back then, you were on your own when the bullies came for you. No day in court to face your oppressors. No press coverage, Facebook backlash, or college scholarship as reward for abuse taken.

My classmates didn't like Mary. "You have dirty blood. Stay away from us, Dirty Blood."

Mary was the picture of neglect. Every day she wore the same dress—stained and rumpled. Shoes bound to her feet with rubber bands. Even in January, Mary had no coat. No mother lovingly ran a brush through her drab hair. Instead, a pair of blunt scissors were used to chase out the lice in her matted, tangled curls. At seven years old, Mary already had the haggard look of someone coming to the end of her days.

Mary never complained about life at home or the torment at school. Mary was as gentle and kind as she was neglected and bullied. When "Dirty Blood" was hurled at her, Mary silently stood and waited for her tormentors to stop.

She was made of sturdy stuff. Never missed a day of school. I turned away from our classmates and spent time with only Mary. In my eyes, Mary was someone to admire, not shun.

Years later, two school bullies turned their fire on me. The bullying wasn't just verbal. I still carry a physical injury from one attack. The memory of Mary's courage in the second grade held me close during my terrifying year of being bullied. That, and the words of the Persian poet Rumi: *In the blackest of your moments, wait with no fear.*

A POSTSCRIPT

Mary didn't return to our school after the second grade. I never got the chance to say "goodbye" and to know if the bullying became too much for her or if her family simply moved away. But I've never forgotten Mary all these decades later, and the lesson she taught me about the power of silent dignity in the face of cruelty.

— 17 —

SIGNATURE NOTE

Roosters still snooze as I perch atop a clothesline pole in our backyard singing songs from *The King and I.*

I'm mesmerized by Deborah Kerr's British accent in the movie— a soft sound so different from my Texas twang. Long after I get too big to shinny up that pole, I still want to "sound British," so I head to London and earn an MA in Voice Studies at the Royal Central School of Speech and Drama. Finally, I can speak posh British—kind of. There's always a bit of the Texas drawl lurking near the surface, wanting to bigfoot my newly acquired accent.

But I learn something more important than a British accent at university. I discover what the Brits call your "signature note." One renowned voice coach there says it's the note we cry out in when we're born—a sound as individual as our fingerprints. When we're grounded in our signature note, we're centered in who we truly are. People are automatically drawn to us when we speak because we're speaking from a place of authenticity. It's a real barrier breaker when it comes to connecting with others. Sadly, the stresses of life slowly disconnect us from this note. A good voice coach helps you unpack the tension covering up your magical note.

Some days at university I suspected my signature note was playing hide-and-seek as I cleaned house to find it again. I think it was miffed about all the stuff I'd piled on top of it. But when you meet up with your signature note again, nothing short of a miracle happens. You're reconnected with what Mother Nature gave you when you were born. And when you speak, it's as though your soul is breathing fresh air out into the world around you.

FINDING YOUR SIGNATURE NOTE IN A PRINGLES CAN

*Finding your signature note is a wonderful kind of scavenger hunt that takes you on an amazing adventure. I found my signature note in a Pringles can (sans the chips.) While on this expedition, I discovered a poem that guides us in speaking in a rhythm that is like catnip to your listener's ear. Folks can't get enough of hearing you speak, and they'll keep coming back to hear more. I invite you to go to my website **www.global-cowgirl.com** to learn about how to find your signature note and how to begin speaking in the rhythm that will captivate your audience and make them perk up and listen to what you have to say. This rhythm, by the way, is the beat that most successful broadcasters and program hosts speak in.*

— 18 —

EVEN A PORTA-POTTY'S PART OF THE THRILL

Give me an Erector Set, and I can put together a building that'll topple right over. But my pathetic track record in attempts at building has never stifled my passion for watching the magic show at a construction site.

Where I live, tall structures are going up everywhere, so each day brings a new thrill. Our town's gone from far-flung outpost to posh metro community enjoying the spoils of government contracting. We are even chosen as the location for a sexy fictional murder on a mega-rated TV crime show. Once your town hits prime time, the sky's its only limit. Of course, hitting prime time means people are now paying prime cash to call our town home. Town fathers are yelling, "All aboard," as we jump on the Equity Express.

Perched in my doctor's high-rise office, I watch another building going up. They've dug out its Bigfoot footprint. Lots of Bobcats, Caterpillars, and alien pieces of equipment scurry in every direction. Each knows its part in this magnificent staging of engineering choreography. The superstars are the gigantic cranes hoisting concrete and metal to support the final structure. The majesty of what they do leaves me breathless. But I'm just as mesmerized by the exuberant bit players bustling around them.

Suddenly, I catch a glimpse of a lone player coming from the wings. It's clearly a machine on a mission. But what's it doing all alone, away from the others? And what's it got clutched in its grip?

It's a blue Porta-Potty.

I can hear cheers and whistles coming from the audience of construction workers. Unfazed, the little machine scoots across the field of dirt, puts down its cargo, then hustles itself offstage—stealing the show.

— **19** —

FOUNTAIN OF YOUTH

"Step right up. Take a dip in the Fountain of Youth. Lie about your age. *Add five years!*"

Once you pass the halcyon age of thirty-five, that golden mean in time when we women are at our dewiest and sexiest, you start wishing clocks traveled backwards. You no longer yearn to reach a future time where you can drink, vote, smoke, drive a car, or have sex without someone waving a placard about your underage promiscuity.

It's at that age I discover the Fountain of Youth. I'm standing at a cosmetic counter mulling over backward-running timepieces that will, hopefully, prevent the impending wrinkles and sags that are to be my future for the next sixty plus years. As my family's expiration dates are usually at about one hundred years, I know my face and I are in for quite a slog in our quest to defy gravity.

The salesperson chirps, "What can I help you find?"

"Something to stop the stride of time on my face."

"How old are you?"

Counter-intuition jumps in. "Forty."

"Reeeaaally? You look fabulous!"

Suddenly, whenever I can weave it into the conversation, I even tell strangers I'm forty years old. And every time, I hear some version of, "You look marvelous, darling. Keep up whatever you're doing."

So, for thirty-five years I've kept it up—adding five years to my age.

Here's what's amazing: The longer I do this, the more the years keep ticking off my face. Now that I'm cuddling up to seventy, the more myopic folks, glancing down at my late-in-life stomach (should have exercised more between bouts of lying about my age) ask, "When's your baby due?"

Never offended, I say, "Thank you for thinking I'm young enough to get pregnant." And then they ask the secret of my youth.

HARD TIMES. PURE LOVE.

Mom's little ones don't have any toys. Not much of a place to call home either. Being a single mom living on the streets with three kids takes a special grit. And you'll never see a mom more determined to show her babies the same love, care, and happiness the most privileged youngsters might have.

Every night I sit by the glass wall at the restaurant in my hotel in Muscat, Oman. The days are baked in heat over a hundred degrees, but by the time I sit down for dinner in the evening, the temperature is safe for kids to come out and play. And every night Mom shows up with her family to let them play and scamper on the sidewalk by my window.

She sits silently, keeping them safe as they chase each other up and down their sidewalk "playground." They have pretend scuffles. They play hide-and-seek behind the building's pillars, jumping out from their stone hiding places to the glee of their surprised siblings. And when that game gets boring, there are always lightning bugs to chase.

Kids being kids, one might play too rough and suffer the retaliation of an angry brother or sister. But Mom quickly steps in to set things right. This mom is 100 percent present for her kids. She doesn't let the weight of their hard life dampen and sadden her youngsters' precious childhoods. She relishes the joy of having them in her life. And she never misses a night bringing them out to play.

This mother cat gives her little feral kittens the happiest childhood she has within her power to give. Their circumstances are hard, some days even dire. But when night falls, everyone comes out to play and enjoy being a family.

— **21** —

YAMMERING

Yammering is a high-paying profession these days. If it were a sport, it'd be an Olympic event. I wonder what would get you a score of 10.0 in this event. Judges' ears being completely chewed down?

This weird wondering pops into my head in a doctor's office. There's a TV monitor perched on the wall of the waiting room. It typically streams stuff to keep patients' minds off how late the doctor's running. Usually the video features a single yammerer standing on a darkened stage talking to an enraptured studio audience. The yammerer's *Jeopardy*-quick thumb clicks from one monument-sized slide to the next while making her points.

I confess, I love yammering. I'm not a pro with an agent, just an amateur who spends a lot of time practicing my yammering skills with friends.

I look up at the screen. *Wait! Where's the yammerer?* I yelp to myself.

There on the TV is a dog sleeping. It's a corgi. He's in a sunny room lounging on a big blue cushion surrounded by fuzzy toys—paws outstretched toward the camera. Each paw takes turns with the occasional twitch. His full belly slowly lifts and lowers with each breath. He's relaxed and silent. I'm transfixed. I want to be that dog.

Now, every afternoon I take a yammer-break, from my own and everyone else's. I close my eyes and run that dog video in my head. It's my midday nap time. This break always makes me think of something Barbara Jordan (a now-deceased congresswoman from Texas) said: "Think what a better world it would be if we all, the whole world, had cookies and milk about three o'clock every afternoon and then lay down on our blankets for a nap."

Now that should be an Olympic event—summer and winter.

SANTA DOESN'T CARE IF YOU'RE TPT

Everything's turned into an abbreviation today. But even as an abbreviation, TPT is a hateful brand to put on people. Trailer Park Trash.

I've sat in many a meeting where colleagues have liberally thrown this phrase around to describe those who they feel are their professional, economic, cultural, or educational inferiors. A subspecies so low on life's totem pole it's unnecessary to feign political correctness when speaking about them.

One day a colleague uses TPT to describe a family who'd lost everything in a tornado. She cradles her superior contempt for these folks like a beloved child. I turn and say, "My grandparents were Trailer Park Trash."

Oops. My colleague babbles some puny excuse attempting to justify her contempt and bigotry. I go on: "Granddaddy was a migrant worker in the Texas oil fields. Moved his family wherever there was work. Long days. Little money. No benefits. Often, home is a spot alongside the road or a company shack with newspapered walls to keep out the North Texas cold. When times were *good*, my grandparents lived in a heated trailer. Being what you call Trailer Park Trash was a step up for them."

I go on: "When I was five years old, we spent Christmas with my grandparents. I told Santa where I'd be and that I really wanted a basketball.

"I still have the picture taken of me beaming with the basketball Santa left for me under Grandmother and Granddaddy's Christmas tree. Behind me? My grandparents' rented trailer.

"That Christmas in that trailer park is one of my happiest memories. The good news? Santa sees people differently than you. Santa didn't see a little girl he thought was Trailer Park Trash. He saw a little girl who believed there really is a Santa."

Me with my basketball and my grandparents. Santa didn't have a chimney to come down into the trailer, so he came through my grandparents' hearts.

FROM ORPHANED AT THREE TO HIGHEST-PAID WOMAN IN AMERICA

Today's Overlord of Narcissism demands young women hire hair, makeup, and clothes stylists even to go to a baby shower, so they'll look "Ahhhhmaaaaayzing" in everyone's photos and in their selfies. No doubt there's an app to paint in the perfect contours they want on their faces. And since shoes now make or break you as a "wonder woman," six-inch heels are compulsory.

Lately, I've been reading about the Hollywood Golden Age actress Barbara Stanwyck. Known more for her husky voice and panther's stride than for her beauty, a young Stanwyck shunned caring about how she looked on or off camera. She let what was happening inside her "paint" the contours of her face. Where did Stanwyck stand on shoes? She once told a costume designer, "If they are looking at the shoes, everything else is a mistake."

Orphaned at the age of three and no real place to call home, Stanwyck took what she had on the inside to become the highest paid woman in America in 1944. A "tomorrow woman" ahead of her time, Stanwyck started a foundation to help women get ahead in business. She herself spurned the Hollywood system, refusing to be "owned" by one studio, as the other megastars of her era were. Stanwyck called her own shots. And when her hair turned prematurely gray, she left it that way and continued to be nominated for Oscars and win Emmys.

Without one acting class, Stanwyck went from Ziegfeld Girl to movie dynamite in films like *Stella Dallas*, *Double Indemnity*, and *Sorry, Wrong Number*. A Stanwyck character surfaced from a deep space within her. This is what brought Stanwyck box-office appeal and award-winning acclaim—not hair, heels, or makeup.

LESSON

Let the "inside you" light up the "outside you."

—— 24 ——

STARTING OVER

Having to sell my autographed copy of *To Kill a Mockingbird* to pay rent still makes my chest clinch.

Staring into an ATM screen showing zero dollars in my account is the scariest moment of my life. More than the teenager putting the gun to my head in Cairo. (Story 12)

I've got a stack of t-shirts declaring, "I've Survived and Thrived."

There's no one to blame but myself for all the rain of frogs visited upon me. When I was three years old, I'd perch in the mimosa tree in our front yard and talk to God. But talking to God's tricky. Choose your words carefully.

I asked God for an interesting life. The inspiration for this prayer? Daddy. He worked at a job he hated to support the family he loved. The interesting life he could have had as a writer was a dream never reached.

Well, God answered my prayer. When I close my eyes for the final time, I can say my life has been "interesting." Problem is, God and I weren't on the same page when it came to an interesting life. Overcoming tough times, back slides, illnesses, and injustices. All character-building, but not what I had in mind when I was a three-year-old perched in that tree.

As I write this, the world is reeling from the Covid-19 pandemic. It's one giant frog storm and too many of us will be starting over—in more ways than we'd welcome.

The good news? I'm a testament to the possibility of surviving a storm of frogs and then thriving. Yep, sometimes it's gonna be about as much fun as pushing a pea up the side of Mt. Vesuvius with your nose, but you'll reach the top. Like me, you will survive and thrive.

— 25 —

SELFLESSNESS

Be selfless . . . be free.
　　　—Swami Sivananda

My aunt died recently. Uncle Buster, no doubt, is perched by the Pearly Gates waiting to give her a big "welcome home" hug.

In my memory, Aunt Trudy is as calm and serene as Uncle Buster is exuberant and feisty. Their marriage is the perfect alchemy of opposites coming together for a beautiful life.

They fall in love in the shadow of the Second World War. For sure, my uncle fancies Aunt Trudy because she's pretty, loves to dance and travel, and plays cards with a vengeance—and she's smart. But I suspect a deeper reason for his love. A reason as old-fashioned and out-of-fashion as giving someone a friendly wave when they let you switch lanes ahead of them in traffic.

In high school, Aunt Trudy is class valedictorian—a placard people like to buff and polish long after they've walked across the stage to get their diploma and give their speech. Not my aunt. I never know about her accomplishment until her funeral. But that's not the whole story.

She gives up her bragging rights about graduating valedictorian. Money for college tuition comes with the title, but Aunt Trudy decides to take a job right after high school. College has to wait. The school principal tells her the salutatorian wants to go to college in the fall, but doesn't have the money for tuition.

"Trudy, would you mind giving up being valedictorian so the salutatorian can have the title and get the money?"

Aunt Trudy says, "Yes," and so can never lay claim to her achievement again. When she does go to college later, the money is no longer hers to use.

My aunt understood the quiet rightness of selflessness. Uncle Buster loved a wonderful woman.

— 26 —

ILLEGAL ABORTION

"Get yourself pregnant and I'll kill you and the baby in your belly."

Josie's daddy doesn't mince words, and he's also a man of his word. Nearly twenty years of living under his roof taught Josie that. So, when she gets pregnant before saying "I do," Josie rightfully fears for herself and her child. Even if she manages to keep her condition secret until late in the pregnancy, she wonders, *Can doctors save the baby after its soon-to-be-granddad beats me to death? And who will take care of the baby?*

It's the 1960s. A time when the law seldom takes the side of a female against an irate father, husband, or any other man. Josie feels cornered into having an abortion even though it's illegal and not every "helping hand" is a clean one. Fevered and weak from a raging infection after the abortion, Josie searches for a doctor to kill the infection before it kills her.

"I'm sorry," every doctor in her small town says. "It's illegal to save you. It's only legal to let you die. The state will take my license for any participation in an abortion. Even after the fact. Helping you puts me in the same bucket as the butcher who did this to you."

Josie goes to a big city hoping to find help. Finally, a doctor says, "Without help, you'll die, and pretty quickly. I'll do what I can here in the office, but don't tell me your name, and please forget mine. After I'm done, don't come back. You're on your own."

Josie's daddy never found out about her pregnancy, never saw the need to kill her for getting pregnant before getting married. I guess you could say that abortion was necessary to save the life of the mother.

— 27 —

STUFF

I'm living in a tiny apartment furnished with dumpster-diving treasures. Two mangled wicker chairs needing a bit of debugging and a rusted metal table with an equally rusted matching chair. I sleep on an air mattress in a bare bedroom. And there is no svelte, smarty-pants TV. Mine is a stocky, remoteless reject from a friend.

I do spring for a lighted palm tree that stands alone in the center of the living room. Come Christmas, I deck the tree out in festive bling. Not wanting the palm to be alone for the holidays, I invite some special friends to keep it company. A flock of plastic pink flamingos stand one-legged around the tree. Red and green Christmas mufflers wrapped round their long necks.

Why the skimpy furnishings? Two years before, I'd sold all my belongings—a home and thirty years of collected treasures—and headed for graduate school in London, where I was likely the oldest student. Once back in the US with a deflated bank account, that lighted palm, those dumpster discards, and the inflatable mattress were all I could afford. It was glorious.

Now, back in the chips, I have "stuff" again. Proper stuff that needs dusting and polishing. Enough kitchen stuff to overflow a dishwasher. A willowy TV that snaps to attention when I give it verbal commands. And, at Christmas, in the center of my posh digs is a traditional tree piled high with stuff I'm giving to family and friends.

I'm sure these same folks thought I was off my nut when they saw icicles and baubles hanging from the lighted palm tree surrounded by a flock of plastic flamingos, but I can't remember when I've ever felt merrier at Christmas. And the greatest gift that year? Simply living with very little "stuff."

NOTE TO SELF
Time to clear out some stuff, so there's room for even more happiness.

— **28** —

A SERIAL KILLER

I'm in a pro-death-penalty state to interview a suspected serial killer. You can know a lot about someone and still not be prepared for meeting them face to face. As a journalist, I've done my homework and know the man's survived a childhood of grisly abuse, mostly at the hands of his hateful mother who once, allegedly, tried to bake him in an oven. When he grows up, he takes the only path he's been shown—one of twisted rage. He claims to have killed at least 150 people. In a soft voice, the suspected killer tells me, "Sometimes I'd jest swerve my car over and hit 'em as they's walkin' along side the road."

Later, at trial, he's convicted of killing eleven people. In the end, the state's governor saves him from his death penalty sentence, and the serial killer dies of a heart attack in prison.

When I met him for our interview, I had expected to feel revulsion. Instead, I went legless from sorrow—for his alleged victims and for him. Tears welled up in my eyes, and I backed out of the interview room. I didn't see a suspected serial killer sitting there. I saw a tortured, broken child, and I wanted to rush over and swaddle him in the love and care he never received as a boy, to hug away the horrors that scorched all the goodness out of him.

Before going back into the room, I dropped my head and prayed. I prayed for the alleged victims, their families, and their suspected killer. And I prayed for myself, because something dark and shadowy passed through my soul when I met this man, and I desperately needed an unfettered faith in God and His mercy for even the worst among us.

FRIENDSHIP OVER POLITICS

It's the middle of the night. I'm cross-eyed with claustrophobia brought on by the "coziness" of my hotel room in Montreux, Switzerland. Heaped atop this emotional dysfunction is a heart-twisting panic attack. In the morning, I'll be coaching a group of hardheaded, recalcitrant do-gooders who believe their mission to save the world excuses all manner of rude behavior. I'm alone, with an ocean between me and home. All in all, I'm in a pretty negative space.

Time to phone a friend—Celeste. We are each other's lifelines when our roads get rocky. More specifically, Celeste (and her husband) is my ask-the-universe-for-help lifeline.

While it's the middle of the night for me, it's not too late to call Celeste in New Jersey, share my angst, and ask her to send me a prayer. She does. Within moments I'm fast asleep. Released from the misery I'd been buried under moments before.

I later tell Celeste she needs to pitch a big tent and share her unfettered connection with prayer with the whole world.

In today's political climate, Celeste and I are unlikely friends. Our political posts are so far apart, we often laugh that one of us is to the left of Trotsky and the other to the right of Attila the Hun. Trotsky and Attila might be an exaggeration, but not by much. But Celeste and I never let politics ruin a beautiful friendship. When I die, it's Celeste who'll tie up the loose ends of my life and take my ashes wherever I want them thrown on this earth. I trust Celeste with my life and my death.

— **30** —

A SUPER MAN

Even standing quietly on a subway platform in Manhattan, Christopher Reeve is an attention grabber, and not just because he's famous. At first, heads whip round in his direction because Reeve is so beautifully tall. But there's something else. Reeve exudes an ease of spirit that cloaks him in a glowing Light.

Years later, I am asked to interview Reeve after the horse-riding accident in Virginia that left him paralyzed from the neck down and dependent on a machine for his next breath.

Walking into his home, I look down a long hallway into a large white room. In the middle of the room sits Reeve in his massive wheelchair looking out a window. Sitting alone, there is a holy stillness about Reeve that commands reverence for what's been stolen from him by the accident.

After the interview, Reeve and I start talking about the movie *Titanic*, which has just been released. Turns out, Reeve is an RMS *Titanic* aficionado.

As we chat, Reeve, now inhabiting a body rendered pale and lifeless by fate, takes on a glow that brings back the color to his skin. The more animated his voice, the easier it is for him to speak, and the brighter the Light coming from him. It's the same Light I'd seen around him on the subway platform years before.

As his connection with the passion he feels when talking about the doomed ship intensifies, out of that Light comes the form of Christopher Reeve before the accident. There are two images emerging from him in that moment. Reeve, that day, in the wheelchair, and the Christopher Reeve we know as Superman. This is the Reeve talking about the RMS *Titanic*. His passion releases the energy and the Light the accident has hidden.

REDEMPTION AFTER SCANDAL

Misdeeds, scandals, and some pretty nasty wrongdoings seem weekly fodder for 24/7 news. Often, redemption, after confession (and maybe a little jail time), comes packaged in a tell-all book, a high-profile interview or two, and, if you're really on the scandal-cash-in express, six-figure speaking engagements that keep you and your agent in the top money-earning 1 percent. In other words, scandal can be a lucrative revenue stream.

Should this be the path most travelled by wrongdoers? The question has me thinking about the Profumo affair back in the 1960s.

No, it isn't sexual harassment that brings down John Profumo, UK Secretary of State for War in 1963. It's his dalliance with a showgirl, who was also sleeping with a Soviet diplomat. Before it's over, Profumo's affair washes a tsunami of scandal over Parliament and the intelligence community and helps bring down the government.

It's reported Profumo, at first, commits a then-unforgiveable offense in British politics. He lies to Parliament, denying the affair. Then he confesses, resigns, and, shortly after, begins working as a volunteer, cleaning toilets at a charity in London's East End. He volunteers by either scrubbing the loos or fundraising for the charity the rest of his life. In the end, Profumo's charity work and silence about his misdeed and lie redeem his reputation.

How refreshing would it be to see those who've wronged country, victims, or family do what Profumo did? Apologize to everyone, then quietly vanish into the metaphorical woods to spend the rest of your life doing good deeds and *never* speaking about the scandal or making a dime off it.

LESSON AND A QUESTION

Sometimes we do things that seriously damage other people. Damage that leaves skid marks on all their tomorrows. What better way to make amends for your mistake than by not making excuses and accepting the consequences for your action? Make amends when possible and forego shortcuts to forgiveness and redemption. And, because crime sometimes does pay, why not give the riches you earn from a book deal and speaking engagements to the folks or person you've harmed, rather than doing a financial victory lap for yourself?

LEAVE THE RULES WHERE GOD FLINGS THEM

My friend Rima speaks five languages. Not me. When I venture beyond English, Rosetta flings stones, fish babel, and there is definitely *une liaison dangereuse* between brain and tongue when I ask for directions in Paris.

Apparently, I'm meant to be monogamous with English—a passionate relationship introduced to me by Daddy. Each night, when Daddy returned home from his job shuffling papers, he sat in his rocker reading a book or doing a bit of writing himself. There was always a yellow tablet and a stubby No. 2 pencil on his TV tray. Daddy loved words, whether his or those of someone else.

A love of the English language isn't all I inherited from Daddy. When I was two years old, he started schooling me in the notion that sometimes God likes flinging our earthly rules in the trash.

"Especially," Daddy said, "rules meant to beat you down when you're growing up."

Daddy walked his talk every Saturday when working on our family car. From the time my hands were big enough to pick up a wrench, I was his mechanic's assistant. It never occurred to Daddy his daughter couldn't—shouldn't—do anything a boy could, including being a mechanic if I wanted.

Daddy teaching me to fix cars didn't mean he thought I was the short straw because I wasn't a boy. Daddy thought I hung the moon. I had dolls, dresses, and dance lessons. And I also had model race cars, airplanes, and a basketball to go with my little-girl makeup and cow*girl* outfit.

To Daddy, I was sugar and spice sauced with piss and vinegar. He never said to me, "Lean in." He said, "Stand tall—and never live by anyone else's rules. Leave those wherever God flings them."

*Daddy and his
cowgirl mechanic.*

*My truly
amazing Daddy,
posing with a
car we worked
on together.*

*Me at two years
old. I wasn't just
a cowgirl; I was
also a car-girl.*

— 33 —

THE HEART HEALER

My cairn terrier, Angus, died five years ago. It's not the first time I've suffered a dog's passing. But a year after Angus dies my anguish is still so deep it nearly snuffs out my spirit. I decide I need help. And that help comes in my helping Ricky Roo.

Ricky Roo is an orange tabby, fifteen years old when we meet. Needs meds twice a day for a thyroid gone rogue. When Ricky's owner dies, his younger, healthy step-siblings get homes straightaway. Not Ricky. No internet ad, Twitter tweet, or YouTube video showing Ricky doing his cutest tricks captures anyone's heart.

One day, looking at the spot on the back of the sofa where Angus liked to perch, I shudder out a choking sob. Then, suddenly, I decide I want a cat. Actually, I'm not the one who makes that decision. It's my soul. Left on my own, I'd have continued wallowing in my grief 24/7.

When I see Ricky on the internet, I know we're destined to be together.

His eHarmony description would have read: "Loving nature. Quirky personality. Adores a good cuddle. Has been patiently waiting for two years to find the purrfect, long-term committed relationship."

Ricky Roo now stretches out on the back of the sofa where Angus once rested. So many folks had looked past Ricky when he needed a home, and I had no one to bandage the wound and heal my heart after Angus died. Ricky Roo and I are a match made by heaven.

A POSTSCRIPT

Ricky Roo hit his earthly expiration date about a year ago. He healed my heart after Angus. Now, I have 15-year-old Lucy, who thinks of me as her Ethel. Like Ricky, Lucy's a heart healer. She came into my life after another difficult loss. This time a loss of the romantic human variety. What it is about senior cats? They're great at healing your heart and showing you how to move on.

DIANA, PRINCESS OF LIGHT

On the morning of the royal wedding of Prince Charles and Lady Diana Spencer, a procession of carriages pulls up to St. Paul's Cathedral. British royalty step out into a sunny day with cheering crowds. Of course, the crowning arrival is the carriage bringing Lady Diana, the soon-to-be Diana, Princess of Wales.

I have the best seat in the house for Diana's arrival—in an American TV anchor booth across the street. The presenters have their backs to the cathedral and can see the pageantry only on small monitors at their desks. The other producers and I look directly over at the pomp and magic.

When Diana steps out of her carriage, she doesn't disappoint. A brilliant light seems to bounce off the fabric of her wedding gown. My eyelids flutter to block the brightness. I think, *What a remarkable reflection of the sun off her dress.*

But it isn't the light of the sun coming off her dress. With each footstep Diana takes up the stairs at St. Paul's, the light grows brighter. There is an otherworldly brilliance coming from *Diana*, not the dress. Halfway up the steps, Diana disappears. Instead, she has become an iridescent Orb of Light. The crowd is transfixed.

Why aren't the anchors talking about this amazing sight?!

I crane around to glimpse at their monitors. There is *no* dazzling Light—only the sight of Diana in her magnificent gown ascending the steps.

I blink to clear my sight. Looking back at St. Paul's, there it still is—the gently moving Orb of Light. Then the Light disappears through the doors of the cathedral.

My eyes can see the Light. Our cameras cannot.

Thousands of pictures will eventually be taken of Diana. None capture the Light I saw that day.

A LESSON AND QUESTIONS

The Light I saw coming from then Lady Diana Spencer is a Light I speak of often in this book. The lesson I learned the day of the Royal Wedding is that the Light not only surrounds us, it comes from within us. Seeing the Light shining from Diana that day opened me to seeing this Light coming from everyone. Moving through our lives, we are all shining Orbs of Light. However, the Light doesn't show itself in selfies, pictures, social media, or YouTube and TV. I wish the Light would sit down for an interview so I could ask it why this is. And is it the Light coming from us that says we're alive, not our bodies?

— 35 —

DO RIGHT BY OUR KIDS

Growing up in Texas oilfields means Mother's schooling is spotty. She sees no chance of bettering herself. Then an oilman in Kilgore, Texas, hit it big and soon Kilgore was bragging it had the greatest concentration of oil wells in the world. The town decides the kids in the town should have a chance at a better life, so they start Kilgore College, a community college that still exists today. Mother's daddy worked in the Kilgore oilfields, so when she graduates from high school at 15, she kicks up her heels and heads off to college and a better life.

Mother's brighter future means I'm not born at the bottom of life's dog-pile. That oilman changed the lives of countless generations.

Years later I move to a neighborhood in a city where kids are struggling at the bottom of America's dog-pile. Mother managed to wiggle out from under that pile. I wanted to know why so few others do? I didn't learn many answers, but I can tell you one—*food deserts*. Mother had homecooked meals made with fresh foods, so, when the chance for an education came along, she had the brain power to take advantage of it.

How can a kid's brain thrive if their only food options are predigested, nutrient-free food infused with every artificial flavor-enhancer conceived by science? The stores that offer fresh vegetables in better neighborhoods, often only offer foods a grade above roadkill in poor areas. America's racoons probably have more access to fresh vegetables than poor kids.

If a country's judged by how it treats its youngsters, we often won't be said to do right by ours. At least give every child the option of better food choices so they have a chance to survive and thrive.

POSSIBLE SOLUTION

Sometimes only a financial incentive gets companies to do the right thing. Perhaps a healthy tax break for putting healthy foods in their stores in poor neighborhoods will incite them to give kids better food options. I have no doubt the tax break we give these food chains would be more than covered by the kids who wiggle out from under the dog-pile and become the productive, hardworking adults they were born to be.

My mother at her graduation. Mother never met an obstacle she couldn't overcome.

MILLENNIAL HONORS AN ELDER

"Mom and Dad both died of a drug overdose. I was put in foster care. Then Granddad took me in, gave me a real home, made sure I got a good education, and taught me the meaning of the American spirit."

This is Rhonda's back story. I'm coaching her for an interview. What do you say to a panel of life-hardened bureaucrats who've seen the worst humanity can do to itself? That's the squad Rhonda must win over in her interview to secure an appointment to an elite government agency.

Prepping Rhonda for the interview, I ask, "Why do you want this job? Your fancy East Coast degree guarantees you an office on Wall Street."

"I want to make the world a more peaceful, better place."

"Okay, Miss America wannabe, if that's the best you've got, you're not gonna get the crown."

Then Rhonda says, "My granddad. That's why. We lived in Hawaii. He was an immigrant who'd gotten his citizenship. He was a young man when Pearl Harbor was bombed, so he raced down to enlist. While standing in line, the other men shoved and pushed him around and made fun of his bad English and foreign accent and called him some pretty foul names.

"Granddad told me, 'I didn't care. I wanted to go fight for the greatest country in the world. And that's what America is. The greatest country.'

"I want this appointment so I can make public service my career. That's how I can honor Granddad and all he did for me and the service he gave this country."

Rhonda said there wasn't a dry eye on the panel when she said why she wanted the appointment to the agency. Rhonda now proudly serves America and the memory of her grandfather.

— **37** —

MAKING AMENDS TO A WORN PIECE OF LINOLEUM

I want to make amends to a worn piece of brown linoleum I shortchanged in a writing contest fifty years ago . . .

Six of us students bunch around a tiny table in an airless room in our high school. We've each been crowned worthy of entering an annual writing contest. After a few silent seconds, the monitor points and says, "Describe that piece of linoleum tile in the corner."

That piece of brown, worn-down bit of nothing in the corner? Are you kidding me? I've got big thoughts I want to share!

I'm miffed. Grabbing my No. 2 pencil, I write something like, "It's brown, ugly, dirty, and needs to be replaced." Then toss my pencil down in an adolescent huff.

Years later, I still think about that little linoleum tile and my lack of insight and the disrespect I showed it. We don't get worn down, dirty, and sometimes look a little worse for wear from living an aloof life protected from the elements of a hard one. What I've come to know, and was too immature to understand then, is that little ragged bit of tile was part of a team of equally ragged tiles that had seen the bottom side of thousands of students' shoes, giving us a safe and supportive place to walk as we set about learning the skills for making it in life.

My high school is about to be torn down, so the little brown tile is coming to the end of its career and going to be thrown out. Sounds strange, but I wish I could rescue it and give it a new home where it can retire and remember a life well spent.

— 38 —

BEING INTERVIEWED BY BARBARA WALTERS

I was once interviewed by Barbara Walters. Not because I was famous. It was for a job as her off-air reporter and editorial producer. I'd be booking interviews, doing research, and helping write questions for Barbara's news interviews. I confess, I wanted to work on her celebrity specials, but I had a knack for news, so I'd been typecast before we met.

The interview lasted half-an-hour. Barbara didn't ask me one question during the interview. I'm not sure she even asked my name. She did the talking. I listened. At least that's what I thought was happening. But something very different was going on.

Barbara was listening with her *being,* not her ears. It was as though she was shining a beam of energy at me that let her see things about me I didn't even know about myself. The energy coming from her to me was non-judgmental. I felt safe. If she *had* asked me a question, there was no secret I wouldn't have confessed.

As Barbara continued to talk, I felt like the most important person who had ever inhabited the universe. My self-esteem soared. She may have been the one making a million dollars a year, but I was the one feeling like a million dollars.

To this day, decades later, if I'm feeling low about myself, I think back to how Barbara made me feel that day without asking me a single question.

I guess Barbara liked what she "heard" during our interview because I did get the job.

LESSON

I learned from Barbara that listening is a full-body engagement that involves all your senses. Every cell in your body must turn its attention to the person you are speaking with. Your mind must commit to not judging another person, so they feel safe in your presence. Barbara was a natural genius at listening. It's no surprise people just couldn't say, "No," when she asked them for an interview.

BRAIN BREAK

I go wall-eyed. My brain struggles to stop jiggling and hitting the sides of my skull. The other driver does a runner.

In the world of concussions, mine's nothing like the bruising an NFL player's brain takes, but I do lose a year of my life to a pile-on of maladies that leave me unable to work, drive, or risk being around people. The sounds of most voices or accents push my brain into a state of confusion or rage. That speaking habit where people end every sentence like it's a question? That really annoys a brain fighting to get its life back.

The cure for healing the mash-up inside my skull? Minimal contact with computers, mobile devices, traffic jams, and broadcast news. No dealing with cable or cell phone providers about problems with my services—services I shouldn't use anyway if I want to save my noggin. Oh, and multitasking? Off the menu.

Apparently, everything you expose your brain to today is bad for it, so I start watching old Doris Day movies instead of blow-stuff-up blockbusters or the news of DC political shenanigans—real or fake. As no one I know is poised to discover the cure for a devastating disease, I stop checking my emails and texts every nanosecond. And, oh, the sweet relief of excising automated phone systems from my life. Only the threat of being sucked into a black hole of annihilation could make me jump back on that gerbil wheel of torment. Slowly, my brain starts calming down.

Detoxing from technology, traffic jams, news, and incompetent customer service leaves me feeling better than I did before the concussion.

BIT OF ADVICE

Listen to your body. Trust me, it has more common sense than you do. Remember, feelings are not necessarily a test of reality. So, the next time you feel like you need to jump on the computer to browse the internet or check your device for the latest texts, get your body's advice first. Then follow it.

— 40 —

TUCK A DUCK

I get a baby duck for Easter from a friend. No problem, except I'm home from college, which is 1,500 miles away. How am I going to tuck a duck back on the plane? Can the duck live in my bathtub in the dorm? Can ducks be walked on a leash? (Saw that once in the French Quarter in New Orleans.)

First, "duck" needs a name. What about "Daiquiri"? It's a drink that makes you feel warm and fuzzy. Perfect for a cuddly, fuzzy little duck.

Like all ducklings, Daiquiri possesses the mysterious ability to imprint on a species bigger than he. In a duckling's brain, it *is* the species on which it's imprinted. And Daiquiri imprints on my mom—*big time*.

Problem solved. Daiquiri's staying with my parents and working out his imprint issues with Mom, who's soon called the Duck Lady by her neighbors. Daiquiri follows her everywhere. Helping with breakfast. Dusting and polishing furniture. Making the beds. Watering the yard. Daiquiri is a duck secure in his place in the world.

Then the day comes for my parents to go on vacation. What to do with Daiquiri?

As Daddy's had enough of "all this duck nonsense," he decides it's time for Daiquiri to face who he really is. So, Daddy bundles up a squawking Daiquiri, whose raging separation anxiety from Mom kicks in, and the two of them head for the local park and pond.

Turns out, Daiquiri is like the kid who doesn't want to go to the first day of school, but when he gets there and sees all the other kids, he never looks back. Daiquiri hops out of the car, sees all those other ducks, spreads his wings, and waddles away. He's now found his real place in the world.

— 41 —

PRAYER IN SCHOOL. SINNER IN THE MAKING.

"You're goin' to Hell. I hope you know that."

So pronounces my fifth-grade teacher when she discovers the church I attend and the God I pray to. Seems my faith has elastic boundaries when it comes to smoking, drinking, divorce, and dancing. I am a seismic sinner in the making.

This was back when every day at our public school began with a prayer. My soul and its ultimate destination had been a burning source of concern among my teachers and classmates since I entered first grade.

Because this isn't my first time at the Judgment Day Rodeo with a teacher, I know it's best to zip my lips, but I refuse to hang my head in a groveling plea for forgiveness. Instead, I look Mrs. Jacks straight in the eye and hope she can read my mind's lips. *Well, Mrs. Jacks, once again, a load has been taken off my mind. Cuz if you and all my other teachers are the ones going to Heaven, I'm gonna be in damned better company where y'all say I'm headed.*

Mrs. Jacks is long gone to whatever comes after this life, and I've gone on to believe God doesn't give a flying fig about our dalliances with imperfection—hers, mine, or anyone else's. He's into the "F" word—"Forgiveness" with a capital "F." Even forgiving Mrs. Jacks for telling a ten-year-old she was going to Hell because of her religion.

Prayer in school. It's complicated.

— 42 —

TATTOOS

Everyone on the plane to Romania is old, except for my husband and me. I'm not sure why I want to go to Romania. It's the days of Nicolae Ceaușescu, the ruthless dictator of the impoverished country trying to survive behind the darkness of the Iron Curtain.

All I know is something is driving me to see Romania.

The other passengers on the plane are eerily quiet. One lady in the row ahead of us is curious about our being on the flight, so we start talking. As we chat, my eyes are drawn to what I think is a bracelet on her wrist. The sleeve of her blouse keeps shifting back and forth across it, so the piece is hard to make out. Then, when the sleeve falls farther up her arm, I see it isn't a bracelet. It's a string of numbers tattooed on her wrist.

I'm not Jewish. Numbers tattooed on the wrists of prisoners in concentration camps during WWII is something I've only read about in history books. Nothing can prepare you for actually seeing numbers tattooed on someone's wrist. Nothing prepares you for looking into the face of someone who has survived such a horror.

Reading the reaction in my eyes, the lady whispers, "Virtually everyone on the plane has numbers tattooed on their arms. We were forced out of Romania and into concentration camps during the war. Most of us are going home for the first time."

Our two weeks in Romania are spent visiting towns, synagogues, and special places these passengers have kept alive in their hearts. Memories that survived the camps, the war, and the new lives they were forced to build away from their home.

The trip to Romania takes on a holiness still inside me.

LESSON

When your soul speaks, listen. There was no "earthly" reason I should have listened to that voice telling me to go to Romania. My ancestors are a rowdy bunch from Scotland. Our religious roots were watered and fertilized by Calvinists, those religious overlords who believe humankind is a pretty sinful lot. A good weeding was sometimes needed to rid their pious lawn of any Quakers (which is the faith I practice today.) And, no doubt, some spiritual Roundup had to be used to choke out any pesky pagans who cropped up in the yard. All this is to say, I had no ancestral or spiritual connection with Romania. I'm glad I let something greater than myself push me to make the trip there. Seeing the country through the eyes of those forced to leave by the Nazis, forced into concentration camps, forced forever to be reminded of the hell they'd survived by the tattoos on their wrists is something my soul wanted me to be able to bear witness to.

— 43 —

WHAT WILL YOUR GUARDIAN ANGEL BE WEARING?

The homeless man leans against a lamppost. Even a block away, you can see a foul aura surrounding his body.

Now what do I do? Should I say, "Hello, how are you today?" when I walk by? Or should I start looking down at the ground now, so he won't think I'm rude when I don't say hello?

I suspect homeless people rattle us because we think, "There but for the grace of God . . ." And, of course, who'd turn down God's grace?

As I'm set to scurry past, head down, I glance for a split second in his direction. The man's unfocused eyes suddenly lock in on mine. His gaze goes from roving to riveted. And coming from his eyes is the brightest Light I've ever seen. Now unable to look away, I stop and stutter, "Hello. How are you?"

In the next moment I hear a horrific crash. I whirl around, and in the spot where I'd have been walking had I not stopped to say hello is a huge air conditioner. It's fallen from an upper window of the corner high-rise, fracturing and pulverizing the sidewalk.

Seconds later I turn back to the homeless man. He's gone. I whirl around 360 degrees, thinking I'll see him stumbling into the park or weaving down the sidewalk, but he's nowhere in sight.

I can only speculate about who that homeless man really was, but I can tell you I never walk past someone who's homeless without saying, "Hello, how are you today?"

You just never know *where* your guardian angel will show up . . . *what* kind of garb they'll be wearing . . . and *who* they're there to help—if you'll just give them a simple hello.

— **44** —

PRICE FOR HEALTHCARE

Jodi's a "working girl." She practices her profession legally at a brothel in Nevada. She's no spring chicken. As Jodi says, "I'm not a new model."

But Jodi has a drop-dead body that's clearly got curb appeal if she wanted to work the streets. Instead, Jodi commutes from California to Nevada for a two-week rotation at the brothel. At the end of every rotation, Jodi takes two weeks off to be at home with her husband and daughter.

Jodi's job is no secret to her husband. While Mack works full time and can easily support his family under normal circumstances, their circumstances are anything but normal. Their young daughter suffers from a genetic disease that means a lifetime of expensive care. Jodi and Mack have already maxed out what their health insurance will pay for Emily's care. And they've called in all the favors the government has for families in their situation.

Jodi works in the world's oldest profession to cover their daughter's $100,000-plus annual medical bills.

"Our love for Emily lets her thrive," says Jodi, "but my profession lets me pay for the healthcare she needs to survive. Some people—no, most people—likely look down on us for what I do. I'm simply grateful for every day we have with our daughter—whatever the price."

LESSON

Jodi's story reaffirmed a lesson I learned in my earliest days of going to church. If God breathes life into a person, we are obligated here on Earth to take care of them if the need arises. Our country's motto is "In God We Trust." Not making healthcare a basic right for everyone seems like shooting God a rude gesture and poo-pooing His teaching that we are each other's keeper.

MAGA

Lots of "gimme" caps out there shouting President Donald Trump's battle cry, "Make America Great Again." Don't know why, but it always makes me think of Dan, a custodian at a news network where I once worked.

Most of the custodians keep a higgledy-piggledy schedule of their own making. They arrive looking like the dog's breakfast, with bits of their own breakfast stuck to their uniforms. They're as crabby as they are disheveled, kicking over cans of trash, then only half picking up the mess they've made. Protective bin liners are left in a wad at the bottom of cans. Sides of the bins are slimed with festering food and drink. Sit too close to one and the odor will burn hair follicles.

Dan's a different sort. He steps off the elevator at 3:00 p.m. sharp. Big smile. Uniform smartly pressed. Shirt buttoned up. Bow tie perfectly knotted and straight. Shoes buffed to a fine shine.

Dan handles each bin with reverence, removing its contents with surgical precision. He then shakes open a fresh liner, delicately arranging it inside the bin. The final touch is the naval knot he uses to secure the liner so that it doesn't slip down during the next day's use.

One of the bins on Dan's route belongs to our highest-paid correspondent. She and Dan have something in common. Both want to be the best at what they do.

Thinking about Dan now, I wonder what America would be like if less time had to be spent sorting out problems with customer service reps because someone upstream at a company only bothered to do a higgledy-piggledy job. What if each of us arrived at work neatly pressed, smiling, and taking pride in doing a good job? Maybe that's how we make America great again.

LESSON

Look for people who do their jobs well and thank them for making America great again. And then look in the mirror at the end of each day and see if you're looking at someone who deserves your thanks.

— 46 —

WHAT SOPHIE CHOOSES

Women of a certain age sometimes turn to the miracles of science when they want to get pregnant. This is the first choice Sophie must make, and with that choice she finds herself pregnant with triplets.

"Would you like to abort one? It'll be an easier pregnancy and much easier raising twins rather than triplets. Which one would you choose?" says Sophie's doctor, who believes in practicalities and practices medicine in a country where such an option is legal.

Sophie, equally believing in a woman's right to choose, looks at the sonogram. Now she must make her second choice. Which unborn child should she choose to abort?

Sophie makes her choice. She is now the harried and proud mother of triplets.

— **47** —

IMMIGRATION

There's a world-renowned surgeon at a world-renowned American hospital whose hands didn't always save lives. As a child, he uses his gifted hands to pick crops in the fruit orchards and vegetable fields on farms in America. He and his parents are "illegals" in the United States. The future surgeon gets lucky. The American immigration system cuts him a break, sees to it he gets an education equal to his genius, and gives him citizenship.

His extraordinary hands have saved at least a thousand American lives so far. His mission to save lives continues. And for each life saved there are children who don't lose a parent, sibling, grandparent, or best friend. A spouse who doesn't lose their life partner. And who knows how many of the people whose lives the surgeon has saved have gone on to make another individual's life better because this once-illegal immigrant delayed that person's expiration date here on earth?

Immigration. It's complicated.

— 48 —

PENALTY. DEATH.

The man on trial for murder never testifies. He never leans over to utter a soft word to his attorney while others testify against him. He's found guilty of murder in a state that takes its justice from the Bible. "An eye for an eye . . . ." Each of us in the courtroom holds our breath. Will the jury sentence the man to "state-sanctioned murder"—the death penalty?

They do.

A force I've never sensed before grips hold of the moment, squeezing all feeling of life out of the room. My chest can't let go of the breath I'm holding. No one moves. No one speaks. Even the family of the victim sits frozen. Mute. No tears of joy. No yelps of victory.

As part of a documentary news team reporting on the death penalty in America, I am curious what motivates jurors to order someone's execution. Especially because statistics show it costs more to put an inmate to death than to give them life without parole. And many states with the death penalty have very robust murder rates. So, the death penalty makes no financial sense and doesn't necessarily keep citizens safer.

I interview a nurse and a rabbi from the jury.

The nurse says, "The decision was wrenching because my profession centers on saving a life. If that murderer came into my ER, I'd do everything to save him. But after getting on my knees and asking God what to do, I felt at peace giving the man the death penalty for his crime."

The rabbi explains, "I believe sometimes the only way you can be saved for taking the life of another is to pay with your own. I believe the death penalty on earth will save this young man's soul in eternity."

LESSON

It's okay not to know who is right and who is wrong on this issue—or on any issue. Some debates will always be with us.

— 49 —

CHESTER

Chester is a cat found nearly frozen to death in a park in New York City in deep January. A local rescuer finds him. Chester's fur is all white. The pictures of him just after his rescue are tragic. He has blackened, matted fur from goodness knows how long living rough on the streets. He has no front claws, and his squatted hind legs and crouched shoulders tell a story of unimaginable terror embedded deep in his body. His eyes are glazed over from a fright only he can see.

I decide to adopt Chester. He is so close to death. He deserves to know love at the end. Within a few days, that glazed look begins to leave his eyes. The terror and heartache of the past appear to lift away from his damaged spirit.

One morning, Chester wakes me with the brush of his nose against my face. He has the most beautiful aura of moist Light surrounding his head. The glow looks delicate enough to blow away with a gentle puff but is, in fact, so dense it blurs Chester's features. Only the softest form of his face can be seen through the Light. He's perfectly healthy. There is a smile in his eyes and a look of love. I can't believe what I'm seeing. Every physical and emotional pain Chester has suffered is gone. Evaporated. The Light around him is pure white, even whiter than his now beautiful, pristine fur. He is haloed in an air that sparkles with iridescent flecks of Light.

Then, suddenly, Chester looks as he had the night before. His emaciated body, slackened skin, and ratty fur are back. The Light is gone. But there is still that deep look of love coming from his eyes.

Chester dies two days later.

LESSON
Sometimes all you can do is accept that what's happened is going to make you cry for a long time. Realize you did the best you could. And hope someday your crying stops.

— **50** —

WE ALL COUNT

"People like you don't count."

That verbal pus oozes out the mouth of someone who works for me. She's miffed. I've hired someone who, unlike her, hasn't attended "the right schools."

After a stare down, I rattle, "The person's hired. It's done."

Adjusting the silver spoon in her mouth, she proceeds to explain again, "You just don't get it. People like you two don't count. You're irrelevant. Nothing you do will ever matter."

My boss, also this woman's mentor, shares the same attitude about my ilk. I'd only managed to elbow my way into their occupational "club" because, if they didn't hire me, the competition would have. There's no telling how miserable a street-fighting scrapper like me could make their lives if I worked for the competition.

It's so easy for any of us to find someone to look down on. Like the homeless men who line the street where I walk going home every night from work. Each is in a varying stage of drug or alcohol stupor sitting inside his makeshift tent or on his cardboard mattress. At first, I'm afraid of them and make my own judgments about their lives.

Then I notice each one always says "Hello" as I pass. Not meaning to menace. Just to say, "Hey, I know you. I see you every night. And I can tell you see me."

One night, a newbie in their tribe makes a rude remark as I go by. Then he jumps to come for me. In a flash, all these men, who've clearly drawn the short straw in life's lottery, leap up to put him down and protect me.

Each of those men count in my life, and what they did that night matters.

— 51 —

KEY TO BEING HAPPY

Competition + Jealousy + Comparing Yourself to Others =
Unhappiness.

So, what is the magic formula for happiness? I found it in the following story[1], and I read it every night before I go to bed.

A King . . . went into his garden one morning to find everything withered and dying. Standing near the gate, there was an old oak tree; the King asked what the trouble was. The oak told him it was sick of life and determined to die because it was not tall and beautiful like the pine, but the pine was disheartened because it could not bear grapes like the vine. The vine wanted to wither and fade away because it could not stand straight and grow as fine a fruit as the peach tree. Even among the flowering plants, the geranium was upset because it was not tall and fragrant like the lilac, and so on throughout the entire garden.

Coming upon a little daisy, the King was pleasantly surprised to find its bright face lifted up, as cheery as ever. "Well, daisy, amidst all this discouragement I am happy to find at least one brave little flower. You do not seem to be in the least bit disheartened."

The daisy replied, ". . . I am happy because . . . I knew you wanted a daisy, so I am determined to be the best little daisy that I can be."

Reading this story each night lets me fall happily asleep and wake up in the morning feeling refreshed as a daisy and ready to be the person I was created to be.

---

[1] Swamini Krishnamrita Prana, *Smiling Within* (San Ramon, CA: Mata Amritanandamayi Center, 2015), 65–66.

— **52** —

A GOLDEN MOMENT

The place I keep picturing in my head and the hunger to find it won't go away. Eyes wide open or shut, the image of standing on a porch looking out at a lake pesters me. But I have no idea where it is. Then my yearning stops.

But the peace doesn't last. The words "on golden pond" become an incessant mantra in my head. Is the voice talking about Squam Lake in New Hampshire, where they shot the movie *On Golden Pond*? Once again, the voice stops as suddenly as it came.

One day at a bookshop, I trip over a book that seems to fling itself from the shelf. *Cabins in Maine*. Hmmm. I decide to buy it. I do need a vacation. However, as it's already well into summer, I'm not likely to get a reservation anywhere. But hey-ho, I'll give it a go.

"It's odd," the reservations manager says, "we've just this morning had a cancellation from someone who hasn't missed coming here in years."

She can tell I'm not local, so she adds, "You know, this is the *On Golden Pond* lake you're coming to."

"Oh no," I counter, "that's Squam Lake in New Hampshire."

"No, dear, that's where they shot the movie. This is the real lake the family came to."

I arrive at the cabin well after midnight and fall into bed. The next morning, I walk out onto a screened-in porch overlooking a lake. I find myself standing on the porch and looking out at the water I've been seeing in my head for all those months—the real *On Golden Pond* lake. (Great Pond, Belgrade, Maine.)

My mind gives in to the silence at the lake, taking in where my soul has yearned to come.

PRISON'S DARKNESS. GOD'S LIGHT.

Whatever you think you know about prison, being inside one puts right all the misconceptions you may have.

By heaven's good fortune, I don't find myself walking down the corridor of maximum-security cells because of a sentence given to me. I'm there working on a documentary about the death penalty. Eyes peer out from six-by-nine-foot concrete and barred enclosures. Groans. Teeth-sucking. Hyena laughs. My ears hurt from the sounds. An inmate catches my eye. Drool and spittle roll down a face scarred by a demented stare. His crazed look skins me of my defenses. He flails his arms out between the bars, making filthy gestures. Even with the bars separating us, I'm terrified for my safety.

The exercise room, prison yard, and even the old electric chair that's no longer in use are open to our cameras.

"What about the prison chapel? May we see it?" I ask. With a shrug, the warden motions to follow him.

Confusing twists and turns dump us out into a dark room. At the front is a movie screen. I don't know when I've seen such violent images in a film. The room is packed with prisoners laughing, stomping, and whistling at the afternoon's entertainment.

Moving across the room, the warden then shepherds me into a small space filled with sunny, iridescent flecks of Light. We are in the chapel. For a moment, I bristle that prisoners must walk through a room of violence to get to a place of worship. Then, a tapping from my soul reminds me we all walk through darkness to get to God. His Light and the chapel are right where they need to be—next to the darkness—waiting to be seen.

THINK ABOUT IT

Rather than allowing prisoners to watch violent movies, why not allow them only to watch G-rated films and TV shows. That would either soften their violent natures or make them never do anything again that would mean going back to prison and having to watch Bambi *for the umpteenth time. That may sound like an LOL, but I'm actually serious.*

— 54 —

A WISH GRANTED

It's never easy watching someone you love wall themselves inside a self-induced hibernation to escape the raw cold of a setback. Ruby feels inadequate to help Sam, who's curled up and living off the fat of better days, waiting for his personal winter to blow over. She longs to be there for Sam but suspects the setback has left him feeling undeserving of anyone's help, especially hers.

Ruby does the only thing she knows to do. She writes Sam a love letter:

> My dearest Sam,
>
> I've been granted many wishes in my life, but there's one wish I never expected to be given, and the one I most wanted—falling in love with someone. You've granted me that wish. Every morning when I wake up, and every night when I shut my eyes, I see your face and realize I've been given the gift of falling in love. Given the gift of having someone to write this love letter to. Given the gift of calling someone "My dearest." Sam, please know . . .
>
> My eyes never tire of seeing you.
> My ears never tire of hearing you.
> My heart never tires of loving you.
>
> My warmest love,
> Ruby

A few months later, Ruby and Sam go their own ways. Ruby's love just wasn't enough.

— 55 —

FULL-BODY SMILE

There's a surefire way to bring a smile to your whole body and let you light up any room—even on your darkest days. I learned this bit of magic when, on the sunny side of sixty, I got accepted into a Master of Arts program at a prestigious drama school in London.

By the way, I managed to do that with no acting experience. So, the next time you decide to look down on yourself and say you can't do something, remember, not everyone sees you the way you do. Just go for what you want and see where you land.

Here's the exercise:

Every time you walk through a doorway into another room, imagine that room is full of people giving you a standing ovation.

Do this when you walk into the bathroom. Bedroom. Going from the living room into the dining room. Into the kitchen. Hear the roar when the garage door opens or when you visit the supermarket.

Don't forget at work: Entering the building. The elevator. Your office or cubicle.

And especially when you're going into a difficult meeting with someone (or a group of folks) who gets up your nose and you're anticipating a battle.

Notice the smile that comes from inside when you imagine that applause. Feel your body stand taller and the muscles around your mouth turn upward.

Consciously and consistently do this for two weeks, whether you're feeling happy or sad. After that, you'll be like one of Pavlov's dogs. Every time you walk into a room it will unconsciously trigger the memory of applause, and you'll break out into a full-body smile without thinking about it.

This exercise is going to change the way you see the world and the way the world sees you.

RISK-TAKER FOR LOVE

I'm a risk-taker. Not the bungee-jumping variety, although I did once fly in a WWI cloth plane with a fishing bobber and piece of wire hanger as the gas gauge.

No. My risk taking is about risking everything to do something I love. They say, "Follow your passion and the money will come." Not necessarily. Especially if the brass ring you're grabbing isn't attached to an MBA or STEM job. But when I was three years old, perched in a tiny mimosa tree in our front yard, I looked up at the big Texas sky and promised Heaven and myself always to do what I loved, no matter the cost.

My bank account is a testament to the financial folly of keeping this promise to myself. I love writing, journalism, and the arts. Not always big money-making professions. I certainly drained the piggy bank when I went to get an MA in Voice from a drama school in London, where I was likely the oldest student. I loved every minute of it, and that venture means when I stand at the Pearly Gates facing my Maker, I can say, "I had a damned fine time in the life You gave me."

Where did my risk-taking gene come from? My great-grandma. Her family's home in Virginia was palatial. Mother claims they were the biggest landowners in the county. Great-Grandma fell in love with a field hand and married him. Got disowned. With nothing, they left for Texas. Following her heart, she became a cowgirl whose life went from pampered tenderfoot to rugged pioneer. Great-Grandma gave up everything for a life with the man she loved. I'm proud of what I inherited from her—the courage to follow my heart, no matter the risk or cost.

A QUESTION

Life is a risky business that demands an answer to a question once posed by American poet Mary Oliver, "...Tell me, what is it you plan to do with your one wild and precious life?"

— 57 —

AGING AND CHANGING WITH GRACE

Jessie was one of the country's first women intelligence operatives. I only meet her once, but that's all it takes. I want to live life Jessie's way. Not the exciting bits, of which there are many, but the time after, when the mundane became Jessie's every day.

What I admire about Jessie is how she dealt with the kind of changes most of us whine and grouse about as we get older.

Jessie lives a lean and Spartan life that takes her to Washington, D. C., and then around the world during the Second World War and after. She never marries and speaks little about what she does. Betsy, her niece, has no doubt Jessie was a spy. Whatever the truth, Jessie loves her work.

Then family responsibilities kick in. Without fuss or fanfare, Jessie walks away from her career and moves to a small town in West Virginia to take care of her parents. Too old to go back to her old life after they die, Jessie retires to an even tinier town in East Texas.

A few years later Jessie has a heart attack. When she gets out of the hospital, she decides it's time to sell her house and check into a nursing home, something most old folks kick up dust about. Not Jessie.

"It's only practical. I live alone. I could have another heart attack, and it might be days before anyone finds me this time."

I meet Jessie after she's moved into the nursing home. When her niece tells me Jessie's story, I decide right then I want to be as unflinchingly practical as Jessie anytime life says to me, "Time to put on your big-girl pants and do what needs to be done next. No self-indulgent bellyaching."

THOUGHTS

When it comes to paying the folks who take care of our elderly, we get tightfisted. Is paying to take care of the people who gave birth to us like having to get tires for your car or eating your broccoli? It's not as much fun as buying the latest piece of technology, or big car, or bigger house, so we go cheap. How do we shift our values? Or do we even want to?

DUCK IN DEMAND

Forty-Nine is in his cage preparing for his close-up. Forty-Nine is a duck in demand. His gigs include flapping for Aflac because he's an advertiser's dream. Loads of charisma, takes direction without argument, never forgets his line, and always wows the audience.

(Not sure why he's called Forty-Nine. Even his backup, should Forty-Nine wake up feeling peckish, answers to a number—Seventy-Six.)

Now, Forty-Nine is the co-star in a feature film. We're interviewing Forty-Nine and the film's director as part of their promotional tour. Jumping out of his cage, Forty-Nine immediately fluffs up his own feathers. No hair or makeup artist needed. Then he calmly lets a member of his entourage put him on the stool where he's to be interviewed.

Forty-Nine is a pro. First, he firmly plants his feet on the stool, owning his space on the set. Then he gives a nod to the cameraperson, showing him his best side. Next, he focuses on the interviewer. Eye contact is crucial. Forty-Nine doesn't take his eyes off her. Finally, he gives a polite quack to say, "Let's do this."

Anyone wanting to win over an audience can take lessons from Forty-Nine. He is the consummate listener. Every time the camera goes to Forty-Nine, you can see, in his eyes and from his body language, he is fully engaged with whomever is speaking. Then, at just the right moment, Forty-Nine offers a perceptive quack.

It's like E.F. Hutton speaking. Everyone turns to listen. Not one to mince words, Forty-Nine follows with a knowing, "quack, quack," leaving listeners mesmerized and wanting more.

So, if you want to exude the charisma and gravitas of Forty-Nine, own the spot where you're standing, listen intently, and speak with only a few carefully chosen words.

— 59 —

WORDS FOR HEALING THE WOUNDS OF THE PAST

Words worth sharing (from *Awaken Children* by Mata Amritanandamayi):

The word *renunciation* scares some people. Their attitude is that if contentment can come only through giving up, then it is better not to be content . . .

. . . Real renunciation is the renunciation of the past and the future. The past is the garbage can where you have dumped all the actions you have performed. It is a storehouse of everything good and bad. The past is a wound. Don't touch it or scratch it. Don't make it bigger. If you scratch the wound—that is, if you delve into your memories—the wound will get infected. Don't do that. Try instead to let it heal. Healing is possible only through faith and love of God. This is possible only in the present. Remember God, chant His name, meditate on His form . . . That is the best medicine to heal the wound of the past. Take that medicine to forget the past, and do not be anxious about the future.

LESSON

Letting go of past wounds means seeing the sun shine again, and you can never have too much sunshine in your life.

— 60 —

JOYFUL BARK. HAPPY ENDING.

I meet Hank when volunteering to feed dogs being starved by their owners in New York City. Hank is a husky living behind a dilapidated building surrounded by a high fence, his fur caked with green mold, his ears eaten down by frostbite and maggots.

Most of the dogs we feed are cowed by life, either crawling on their bellies toward us or growling and pulling at their chains to bite off our hands. Not Hank. When we show up, Hank bounds over like a pup, greeting us with a joyful bark.

Feeding Hank means throwing his food over the high, walled-up fence. One morning, I throw over a really big portion of wet food and then peep through a small slit in the barricade to get a glimpse of Hank. Looking back at me are Hank's piercing blue eyes. He lets out a happy bark despite the fact the wet food has landed smack in the middle of his head, with odd bits clinging to his chewed-down ears. Hank, ever the optimist, just shakes his head and laps up the food.

Then, Hank's fortune changes. He gets rescued, and the next time I see Hank he's got a new family, including a little girl who loves wrapping her arms around his bushy neck and kissing his mangled ears.

It's easy, in the tough times, to get down and count yourself out, to turn into a nasty snapper or lifeless spirit killing time till time kills you. Hank isn't having that. He's got new digs and all the food, water, and love his unflagging optimism can bring. He spends no time letting his past darken his present. Hank just keeps letting out a joyful bark for his happy ending.

MY TAKEAWAY FROM THE STORY

When you feel like life's hiking its leg on you, don't cower or get snappy. Let Hank's wisdom be your guide. Shake it off and know that good fortune is out there waiting for you. And when that good fortune does come, don't wallow in your sad past. Let out a joyful bark for your happy ending.

— 61 —

FAKE BIRTHDAY

Christmas. New Year's. Then a week later, my birthday. *Ugh!*

While sharing a birthday with King Elvis is kinda cool, it's really a crummy spin of the Wheel of Birthday Fortune. Everyone's either partied out or headed for winter vacation, and even with after-Christmas sales, no one's in a gift-giving mood. They're well overspent.

Then there's the winter gloom that settles in. People are ready to snuggle in out of the cold, hibernate, and recover from the holidays. By my birthday, the season of celebration has reached its expiration date.

As a kid, I didn't realize I had the power to set things right. I just accepted my fate. Then the gods invented Facebook, some place where I'm not obliged to tell my real birthday. I can give myself a new birthday, a better one. One in the summer, when the astrological lion roars and other holidays don't obstruct or impede people from giving me parties and gifts. A month when we're not wallowing in SAD (seasonal affective disorder, a type of depression).

I just had my Fake Birthday yesterday. Tons of Happy Birthday e-card alerts ping my iPhone all day long and well into the night. Gifts. Hot dogs at Five Guys for lunch. Then a *Babette's Feast* at some place fancy for dinner. Friends, of course, know it's my Fake Birthday, but they don't care. They like celebrating me on the day I like celebrating myself.

Of course, there's always someone to drop a dead fly into your meal. I'm a woman of mature years. Someone surrounded by their own sphincterness says, "Does this mean you're twice your age because you have two birthdays every year?"

Clearly, this person hasn't lived long enough to understand the thrill of skipping to the beat of your own drum.

— 62 —

APPLAUSE

Elevator door opens. The fellow inside looks me straight in the eye. I can't break his stare. He is shamelessly flirting. The woman with him rolls her eyes and moans, "Harold, stop embarrassing yourself."

Then she says to me, "Please forgive Harold. He's such a ham. He's working you like he used to work the crowds at his shows."

Harold the Ham is a bull terrier, a retired champion show dog. He looks like the Target dog on steroids. After the elevator doors close and I'm Harold's captive, he really gets down to working his act. Harold turns to this side. Then that side. Then he does some attentive sitting. Every moment is focused on getting my approval. I swear Harold even gives me a few winks.

"He misses being the center of attention," the woman with him says. "Hates retirement. There's nothing Harold loves more than doing what he's doing for you now. And the bigger the crowd the better."

I can't resist. I applaud Harold when he finishes his routine, and he laps it up. Shifting from paw to paw, Harold keeps glancing over at his owner as if to say, "See, I've still got it, sister."

"Did Harold know when he won or lost a competition?"

"Don't you know! Winning meant applause and that sent Harold dancing, prancing, and spinning in circles. When he lost, he'd be sad, standing to the side watching another dog get all the applause. Losing was hard for Harold."

I agree with Harold: applause is a real pick-me-up. So now I have a special gift I give myself on days I feel glum. Every time I walk through a door into another room, I imagine a crowd greeting me with a standing ovation. Then something inside me begins dancing and spinning.

NEVER SNUB WHERE LIFE PUTS YOU

I don't like being inside medical gizmos. The one the tech squeezes me into brings on a hateful attack of claustrophobia. I fear that tight space more than the shame of screaming, "Get me out!"

Set free, I stumble back into the doctor's waiting room, where another patient stifles a chuckle. The woman and I are there for the same test. Clearly, she's braver than I, and we both know it. But my hysteria causes us to strike up a conversation. Before I know it, I have a new business client.

That gets me to thinking. All the good things that come my way usually happen in circumstances I'd rather snub.

For instance, I decide to go to graduate school on the sunny side of sixty, then graduate with the bank balance of a debt-indentured twenty-one-year-old. Desperate for cash, I answer an ad for a housecleaner. The interviewer wonders about my skimpy housekeeping experience and says, "Okay. What's your real story?"

Long story short? I end up with a six-figure job offer that's right in my wheelhouse.

But here's the best one. I once lived in a city all about image. Being put at a table by the kitchen at the city's biggest media event is a career killer. The person hosting the event hates me, so there I am, perched at the table by the kitchen. Waiters whiz by. Dirty dishes get chucked into containers just inches from the table.

Then serendipity throws a Hail Mary pass to save my career. The stranger sitting next to me turns out to be a person who gets me hired for a one-of-a-kind job, traveling the world producing interviews with famous folks in the news.

— 64 —

UPENDING WHAT WE THINK IS IMPORTANT IN LIFE

I read somewhere (can't remember where) that our memory gets fuzzy about the *nouns* in our life, those pesky names of the people or places we know like the back of our hand. But we never forget our *verbs*.

You're not likely to think to yourself—or out loud—*What's it called when you move your legs really fast and your feet hit the road opposite each other? Running. Yes, running. That's it.*

You might have a momentary lapse about the name of your coworker who's doing the running, but you don't forget the word "run."

This has me thinking. Conventional wisdom is that the people, places, animals, and things—the nouns of our lives—are most important. But maybe it's the actions we take with the nouns of our life that have the most meaning, and this is the reason we never forget our verbs.

Can it be that our actions—the verbs of our life—should be our primary focus so we can then really upend the state of the world and how it goes around, making it a better place for the people, creatures, and places we love?

POWER OF THE LEMON

Each morning I hold a lemon in my palms. I'm fixated by its "eye" shape. Its exuberant, friendly color. And when I prick the skin to release the lemon's zesty scent, I feel cleansed—scrubbed spotless of anything in my past that could hold me back in my present or future.

I begin every day holding a new lemon. A fresh start as the sun comes up. Cradling the lemon in my cupped hands, I take in its sunny disposition and imagine the lemon possessing the power to fill me with sunshine and to make the new day a sunny one.

LESSON

Mother Nature offers endless and interesting ways to have a better day. Just look around and see what catches your eye. Maybe you'll be looking into the heart of an artichoke.

— 66 —

TEXAS DROUGHT

In Texas, it's all about the weather. Tornadoes. Hail. Hurricanes. Blue Northers. And droughts. A few years ago, the state thought it was the Land God Forgot because the drought had been going on so long. Even the Texas Longhorns, known for scoffing at a drought, had drooping horns. When folks looked at the sky and merciless sun, their faces turned sour, except for Jesse. He beamed back at the cloudless sky and said, "This is a great day."

"Why?" chokes everyone.

"Cuz, we're one day closer to rain."

Now there's a new way of thinking about tough times and how to keep our spirits up, while we're waiting for the bad times to move on.

SECRET TO WORLD PEACE

Everyone looks so cheerful when I walk into the production office for a freelance gig. The air seems to sparkle with their exuberance. I even hear one or two folks whistling while they work. You'd think I'd walked into a cult gathering where they're pushing the Kool-Aid *du jour*, but everyone seems well grounded. No one is spouting canned lingo hailing the attributes of an unseen Oz Head. Just genuine friendliness and happiness floating through the offices.

I settle into my temporary digs. Midmorning, nature gives a jingle, so I head off to the loo. "Toilet" seems too crude a word given what I behold when I push open the door. The swinging portal takes me into an alternate universe. It isn't the plush carpet, travertine counters, or exquisite sinks and faucets that take my breath. Nor the gentle whiff of jasmine from the fresh flowers. It's the lighting.

Forgetting why I'm there, I stand transfixed, staring at the face framed in a beautiful mirror. I am a vision. The angle of the lighting heightens my cheekbones, lifts my jawline, and removes every line and piece of under-eye baggage I've been carrying for years. The light's gentle tint makes my skin glisten.

A river of cocktails, a pile of antidepressants, a massage, gluten-free cupcakes, the vanquishing of all my enemies, or even a squeeze from George Clooney could not lift my spirits more. A millisecond standing in front of that mirror boosts my energy, exfoliates away all self-doubt about my outer and inner beauty, and floats my soul up to our Maker.

Maybe the secret to making everything right in the world is simply good lighting. It's pretty tough to hate anyone or anything when you feel like a million dollars.

TWO QUESTIONS AND A LESSON

Is world peace possible? It's kind of a depressing question, because there's no earthly evidence that it is. So why keep trying? Maybe it's best to consider the words of Annie Oakley for the answer to that question and the lesson in this story, "Aim at a high mark and you'll hit it."

EPILOGUE

BUBBLE OF LIGHT

Throughout *"Don't Put a Cat on Your Head!"* I write about the miraculous Light I see dancing inside every person and in everything around me. It's the same Light that surrounded the young man and me when he put the gun to my head in Cairo, Egypt.

The Light created a bubble of Itself around the two of us. Inside this bubble, I experienced what, in *Star Trek*, Dr. Spock would call a Vulcan "mind meld" with the young man. We became one mind in a situation where mutual trust and understanding were needed, so there could be a peaceful outcome to our moments together. When I had the thoughts, *"If you pull that trigger, will killing me heal the pain that's driven you to this moment?* and then, *"You are already forgiven, even if you kill me,"* our minds had the intimate exchange—a moment of mutual clarity— that was needed to heal the situation.

I cannot overstate the profound effect the experience in Cairo had on me. In that moment, inside the Light, I felt Its power to bring together people from different backgrounds and points of view and help them forge a focused unity and commitment to building bridges over what divides them. Swaddled inside the Light, you can see, hear, and understand another person—and their view of the world—in a way that's not possible outside the Light.

Now, as part of my work as a writer, storyteller and interviewer, I help business folks connect better. To find common ground for agreement rather than always locking horns. To do this, I created a technique I call the *Bubble of Light*, which captures and grounds my experience inside the Light that surrounded the young gunman and me in Cairo. Without fail, this technique creates trust and understanding between people. Where trust and understanding exist, differences of opinion actually become the ingredients for creating new ways to see a problem and forge a solution. No matter how rancid the rancor, or long-standing the disagreement or grievance, everyone involved in the dispute leaves the *Bubble of Light* changed and motivated to mobilize the Solution, with a capital "S," that's been reached after being in the Bubble.

As I write this epilogue, America sits on a powder keg of warring opinions on how best to deal with the issues, grievances, and injustices that divide us. Racism; equal rights to healthcare and education; unemployment in the wake of Covid-19; income disparity; gun ownership; access to fair housing; the best way to cast a ballot in the presidential election. The list is lengthy and growing.

Some days it feels like America, and the world, is on a train headed toward a mountain where no one's dug a tunnel. Our democracy seems on the verge of blowing itself to kingdom come if we don't start coming together to reconnect with the best in our nature as Americans.

Sadly, the problems we're facing now aren't new. Rows and protests over these issues have been with the world for millennia. So how do we find Solutions *today* to these problems before America does itself in?

Given what I experienced in Cairo, I believe we can find Solutions to these age-old issues inside the *Bubble of Light*. The *Bubble of Light* technique taps into the power of the Light and creates an environment where real-world Solutions are possible.

I invite you to go to **www.global-cowgirl.com** to learn more about the *Bubble of Light* technique and how we the people and our politicians, business and thought leaders, activists, community organizers, and news media can use this tool for helping us all to survive and thrive.

USING THE BUBBLE OF LIGHT IN MY OWN LIFE

The beauty of the Bubble of Light technique is that you can use it in your personal life as well.

Humorist Erma Bombeck wrote a book entitled *Family Ties that Bind...and Gag!* My mother and I had a relationship that fell into the "bind and gag" bucket. We were not a Hallmark Channel mother and daughter pairing. Getting along was rough from the moment I slid out of her womb. Our words were harsh, and many tears were shed. I suspected when it was time for Mother to pass out of this life, I would be left racked with guilt and wishing for a lot of do-overs.

Mother was mere months from turning one hundred when she got sick. I decided I wanted a peaceful end to our relationship. I wanted there to be no drama and angst between us in what were surely to be her last weeks before dying. So, without telling her what I was doing, I began putting the *Bubble of Light* around us whenever we spoke, even on the phone. I also had imaginary conversations with Mother about old hurts and grudges, while surrounding us in the *Bubble of Light*.

By the time Mother died, the *Bubble of Light* had evaporated all the toxicity between us. All our disappointments from an imperfect relationship had been released. Mother's last hours were spent with me cradling her in my arms. A physical closeness that had never been part of our relationship. Mother died knowing she was loved, and I am left with no regrets and feeling forgiven for my part in the rocky road we had traveled. Inside the *Bubble of Light* healing and peace are possible.

SHARE YOUR STORY

You may never have been silly enough to put a cat on your head, but I bet you've got a story or two to tell, and I'd like to hear it. Each of us brings our own special spice and spirit to the human community. If you'd like to tell me your story or share how you feel about one of the stories in *"Don't Put a Cat on Your Head!"*, please go to:

www.global-cowgirl.com

Let's connect. With all the frills and fineries of today's technology, we can connect no matter where you are in the world.

GLOBAL COWGIRL COACHING PROGRAMS

I've learned a lot in my travels as a global cowgirl, and now I've turned many of these lessons into coaching programs I'd like to share with you:

- How to Increase the Power and Effectiveness of Your Voice
- Find Your Leadership Voice: Power, Style, and Influence
- Use the Power of Stories to Achieve Your Business and Personal Goals
- Accent Reduction for International English Speakers
- Fire Up Your Voice and Show Your True Grit (for Cowgirls only)

I invite you to go to my website, **www.global-cowgirl.com**, to explore what these and other programs can offer you.

WHAT'S NEXT FROM THE GLOBAL COWGIRL

In the next book in the *Stories from a Global Cowgirl* series, I find more true stories and new ways for bringing us together and sharing the experience of simply being human. In fact, I'm establishing a community of folks with stories to share. A community built around the collective belief that sharing our individual stories helps us come up with new ideas for creating a better, stronger world for everyone. I look forward to you joining this community.

I would like to leave you with my favorite quote about storytelling:

We are, as a species, addicted to story. Even when the body goes to sleep, the mind stays up all night, telling itself stories.

Jonathan Gottschall

ACKNOWLEDGEMENTS

I got my first pair of cowgirl boots when I was three years old. I learned pretty quick a pair of boots can take you just about anywhere you want to go, so long as you have people smarter than you to show you the way. Here are the smart folks who gave me good advice and cheered me on as I worked to write this book.

Deirdre Silberstein. She wore many hats on the trail to getting *"Don't Put a Cat on Your Head!"* written, edited, and published. Without Deirdre, this book would have remained just a file on my computer.

Katherine Falk, MD, who taught me the ultimate secret in how to survive and thrive, no matter the obstacle put in your path.

Thanks to the friends who were my alpha and beta readers. Companions in helping me honor those whose stories I have shared. To each of you my deepest thanks: Ronalafae Thapa, Catherine Stevens, Kathryn Turner, Ann Albin, Rafif Jouejati, Peter Shaplen, Lauren Kirby, Helga Buck, Carolyn Bruna, Stephanie Cassidy, and Terry Irving.

Lynn Amos of Fyne Lyne Ventures clarified my fuzzy vision of the book cover art and page design, bringing them to life.

I would like to give a special thanks to Forward Movement for allowing me to use stories I shared with them in their series *Meeting God Day by Day—A Year of Meditations* and *Abiding with God Day by Day*.

Telling other people's stories is a humbling honor, and it is impossible to overstate my gratitude to the folks in *"Don't Put a Cat on Your Head!"*. Because of them my life is richer than I could ever have imagined when I put on my first pair of cowgirl boots.

DISCLAIMER

My stories sometimes do include other people – that's the nature of stories. With the exception of known people I have met professionally, whenever I do mention someone, I have changed the person's name and any details that might identify the person and the situation.

Each of these stories is true and told to the best of my remembering. The situations, incidents, and dialogues represent my experience, thoughts, and interpretation of the events.

ABOUT THE AUTHOR

SUNNY M^CMURTREY was born in Fort Worth, Texas. She got her first pair of cowgirl boots when she was three-years old and hasn't stopped being a cowgirl since.

As a Global Cowgirl, Sunny has been to many places that little cowgirl never imagined she'd go, including Cuba, Egypt, Iraq and the Hanging Gardens of Babylon, Oman, Jordan, Romania, Bulgaria, East Berlin before the Wall came down, and almost every state in the Union. Sunny has called Manhattan, Houston, Austin, Fort Worth, Washington, D.C., Los Angeles, and London home. Never wanting to be fenced in, Sunny hopes to call a few more cities home one day. For now, Sunny lives in Frederick, Maryland, where she's working on her next book and her Global Cowgirl Ventures.

Visit Sunny online at **www.global-cowgirl.com** to tell her your story and learn about her podcast and blog.

Made in the USA
Middletown, DE
28 December 2020

30294023R00068